Overcoming

A Journey From Pain to Peace, Purpose and Power

by

Natasha Ickes-Saman

First paperback edition December 2020

ISBN 978-1-7362897-0-9 (paperback)

ISBN 978-1-7362897-2-3(Ebook)

www.dare-2dream.com

Dedication

This book is dedicated to all the little girls who never felt like they were enough. Who in turn became women who didn't understand their worth. This is for anyone who has ever struggled with low self esteem, addiction or simply not living to their full potential. May we all rise above, be happy and create the life of our dreams.

Table of Contents

Prologue

Even as a little girl, I battled deep feelings and dark thoughts. Back then, I didn't have the words to describe the storm of emotions raging inside of me. My moods could shift from a beautiful calm to a catastrophic storm in the blink of an eye. It seems fitting I am a water sign; my emotions run deep as the ocean. A sensitive Cancer and year of the Tiger to top it off. In my shell, most of the time, coming out to attack when necessary. My moods are something that took me a long time to get under control. As a little girl, I couldn't comprehend what I now know to be depression. It's something I struggled with for as long as I can remember. I'm not sure if it was a chemical imbalance or life's circumstances. The adult me views it as a combination of both, as well as a misguided mindset and perspective. As a child, I just knew that I always felt different. I was a stick-thin, biracial girl with big frizzy hair and an odd last name - Ickes. But it was deeper than that. I was in so much pain I did not know how to process. Pain that, despite my best efforts, stayed with me for years. As an adult, I spent over a decade on a journey of healing and growth. During that process, I had to go back to the beginning, to the hurt, the pain and the past.

Most of my memories begin around the age of 10. Events etched so clearly in my mind that have yet to fade. But through the foggy memory of my earliest years, there are a few things as clear as if they happened yesterday. My parents screaming at each other as I played in my room. Little me confused, eyes wide, trying to pretend it wasn't happening. Being sat down at three as my parents told me they were getting divorced. A concept I was too young to understand. Instead, I picked up on the emotions seeping from them both and took them on as my own— sadness, failure, defeat. Whatever divorce meant I knew it wasn't good. Shortly after my parents separated, I was on an outing with my mother and her new boyfriend, Rickie. We were all standing together in a quiet section of downtown Oakland called Jack London Square. It's a small area of shops and restaurants. A great place to walk around and enjoy the day. The main attraction is that it's right on the water. It's an area I always enjoyed going to as a child. My favorite part is the huge Barnes and Nobles, where I spent hours lost in books. On this day Rickie bent down, scooped me in his arms and sat me on the railing overlooking the water. Until that moment, I felt good. Funny how things can shift. The moment he placed me on the railing, terror filled my body. I clenched my mouth shut and was silent. But my heart was beating fast, my face was hot and my mind was racing. "I hope he doesn't kill me. Please don't throw me into the water. I Am Scared." Quick thoughts I wouldn't let escape my lips. He terrified me.

He was loud, angry and unpredictable. Something about his energy didn't feel right, even to a child as young as I was. What I didn't know at the time was that he was addicted to crack. I didn't know that he would disappear for days on a drug-filled binge, only to return to my mom with whatever was left. Whatever emotions, whatever high, whatever anger. What I did know was that he was mean. I have always been able to sense the energy of others and what was deep inside him scared me to my core. I felt like he was capable of unspeakable things. Things I didn't want to be a witness or victim to. I was scared for my mom and I was afraid for myself. At 3 years old, I so clearly remember it being the first time I thought I might die.

Other events have stayed in the back of my mind, popping up at random times like an unwanted guest. Like when I was 9 years old and pressed a knife to my wrist contemplating taking my own life. Or when I was 17 and took a bottle of sleeping pills before laying down and waiting to die. There are other memories, pleasant and difficult, that we will get deeper into during the course of this book. There always seemed to be this internal battle. These painful mood swings. I went from elated one minute to hopeless the next. I was very sensitive, self-critical, self-conscious and felt deeply misunderstood. There was a dichotomy. Because there were also lots of good things. In fact, for the most part, I would say I was a pretty happy child. I loved school, ice skating and time with friends. I had a cat named Tiger, tons of books and loved riding my bike to Blockbuster and the library. I ate ice cream, played board games and got daily treats from my dad. Because according to him, every day was a special day. It's just that the lows were always dangerously low. There was a consistent feeling of being good enough, not being pretty enough and not being loved. Negative thoughts are like a poison. They swirl through your mind until they break through the surface, usually in an unwanted and unexpected way. Over the years I had so many thoughts of ending my own life. Thoughts I tried to fight through. But I was unequipped. A lightweight in a heavyweight battle. Lacking the tools, perspective and mindset to shift my reality. I was facing this giant of chronic depression with no idea where or how to overcome it. I wasn't alone though. I clung to bible verses like a favorite blanket. I held onto wise words from my grandma like a lifeline. The absolute most comforting thing in my life was that I always felt a deep connection to God. I never looked at God as a judgmental man in the sky. He was an essence, energy and best friend. I can now look back on who I was, what I went through and thank God for it all. I am grateful for a mother who instilled a love of reading and a work ethic unmatched. Where would I have been without a father who was there every step of the way, never wavering in his love, consistency and support. I had a network of family and friends who touched and blessed my life in so many ways. I also thank God specifically for the pain, lessons and failures. I am so grateful for my path, a road map to where I am today. A blueprint designed by God especially for me. Because of that this book is about change, growth and transformation. There is nothing sadder than going through life without changing. We must elevate ourselves, transform our lives and grow. Our past doesn't dictate our future. Our mindset and perspective are what determines where our lives will go. I hope that is what you get out of this. It is just one little girl's story. The story of a child who never felt like she was enough. At the same time, it is the story of a child who kept pushing. Who, despite so many failures and mistakes, refused to give up. And through the refusal to give up, developed a powerful strength. Remember, pressure makes diamonds, so grow through what you go through. This is my story. The story of a person who felt stuck, depressed and unfulfilled until I discovered the secret to turning my life around. It is the story of how I fought tooth and nail to find peace, power and my own divine purpose.

Our deepest fear is not that we are inadequate

Our deepest fear is that we are powerful beyond measure

It is our light, not our darkness that most frightens us

We ask ourselves who am I to be brilliant, gorgeous, talented and fabulous?

Actually who are you not to be? You are a child of God

Your playing small does not serve the world

There's nothing enlightened about shrinking so that other people won't feel insecure around you

We were born to make manifest the glory of God that's within us

It's not just in some of us, it's in everyone

And as we let our own light shine we unconsciously give others permission to do the same

As we are liberated from our own fear our presence automatically liberates others

-Marianne Williamson

$\mathcal{C}hapter\ 1 - \mathcal{R}oots$

It seems like this strange dichotomy has always been a part of my life. Good times tainted by grief and depression. Beautiful moments woven into the thread of insurmountable pain. Ever since I was a child, I went back and forth between two worlds. One of a happy go lucky girl and the other of a lost little soul, hurt and confused. This pattern continued with the birth of my brother. He was so cute. This perfect baby. Chubby with a huge grin, dark hair and the most amazing tie-dyed eyes. They were blue or grey depending on the day and splashed with specks of hazel that I could stare into for hours. I loved him from the beginning. My little Jesse. I envied children with a live-in best friend and at 9, I finally had a brother of my own. I had imagined all the fun things we would do and all the things I could teach him. It was the purest form of love.

At times I slip into a memory I tried to forget. I see myself walking up to the door of Jesse's room. I peer in and observe my stepmother holding him. She has a look of complete adoration. It was such a beautiful moment, yet I was overwhelmed with a flood of different emotions. The corners of my mouth dropped as I was hit with a wave of nausea. My face flushed as uncomfortable emotions ran through my body. Suddenly filled with hurt and emptiness. Shame and guilt as an intense longing took over me. It was something I never felt before, or at least not in this way. Deep in my gut, I had this desperation and desire. I wanted that. That thing that can be sensed but can't be put into words. Because as sweet as she was, I knew she would never love me like that. A fact that had nothing to do with her or her character. She, along with her family, had welcomed me with open arms. They had always been kind, loving and generous. But at that moment, I could see it and I could feel it. That bond between a mother and child. That look of pure love. As an empath, I have always been able to feel the emotions of others. What I felt in that beautiful moment left me empty and yearning. Longing for that bond with my own mother. So many thoughts and emotions rushed me, overwhelming and intense like a dam giving way. It was suffocating and confusing. Where is my mom? Why doesn't she answer when I call? Why do I only see her every other weekend? Why doesn't she look at me like that!? Now it is very possible that my mom did look at me like that. I don't know. But in my 9-year-old mind, I didn't feel that type of love from her and didn't understand why. I was on the outside looking in on something I so desperately wanted. There were great times with my mom. Hours in bookstores, afternoons in museums, exposure to documentaries and lots of holiday gifts. However there was a lack of consistency. Lots of broken promises and painful memories. Countless days, waiting endless hours for her to show up and she never did. So often, calling her repeatedly with no answer. Desperate for her to be there and devastated when she wasn't. Somehow always surprised at the regular pattern. Memories of her drug-addicted boyfriend who terrified me. He was loud, angry and verbally abusive. So much confusion. Why did she work a job in a big fancy office and was the most brilliant person I knew, but lived in a motel and didn't have a car. As a child I thought it was because I didn't matter enough. I wasn't worth more. I didn't deserve a mom who cooked for me and tucked me in at night. I didn't deserve a mom that packed my lunch and took me to school every day. I didn't even deserve a mom that answered my phone calls or picked me up every weekend. I tried but couldn't understand why. Visits to my mom were often short and spaced out. By the time I was 5, my mom had left Rickie and had met the most loving man, Kenny. From there on out the visits to my mom were fun. Enjoyable, despite it being my mom, Kenny and myself in one room overflowing with stuff. The locations changed, but the scene was always the same. Lots of clothes, books and random items. The lives of two adults and an occasional child, stuffed into a motel room intended for an overnight stay. Nothing was private and at times it was uncomfortable. On the other hand, it gave me the ability to easily adapt. As a direct result of those circumstances, it didn't take much for me to feel at home. Despite the benefits I was resentful, hurt and confused. I did not have the maturity to understand that becoming a parent doesn't make you perfect or immune to mistakes. My mother, like all parents, is simply human. She had her own pain and trauma from her childhood, wounds she didn't even know she was still carrying. As I got older, I understood she had her own issues that had nothing to do with me. She was there for me in the best way she was able. As a child I didn't get that. I felt empty and worthless. For the first time, in my dad's kitchen, I didn't want to live anymore. It was odd. A thought that had never crossed my mind now had full control. While my stepmother was gazing at my little brother in awe, I turned and crept into the kitchen. The thoughts had faded, my mind was empty and I grabbed a knife. An old weathered wooden handle with a short silver blade. I stared at it for a few minutes, wondering. If I sliced my wrist, would it hurt. How deep would I have to go? I toyed around with those questions, scared at the possibility of pain. I pressed it against my wrist. I was almost in a daze until the first sharp flicker of pain. At which point, I decided that wasn't going to work. I snapped out of my focused fog, scared at how deep I had gone and stuffed the knife back in its place. I wasn't crying; I was calm. At that moment, I promised myself if I ever went through with an actual attempt, that wouldn't be the way. It would have to be more gentle.

My dad and I lived in a small one-bedroom apartment over a grocery store where my dad worked. It was small but beautiful. Large windows, lots of wood and super quiet. The neighborhood was amazing. Peaceful, clean, lots of trees, surrounded by big houses and rich neighbors. Again, the dichotomy. My dad gave me the only bedroom. He converted the living room into his living space. It was a small studio apartment surrounded by multi-million-dollar homes. But the location was perfect. And my dad working so close meant he was always a few minutes away. I could run to him for anything from boredom to a paper cut. The close proximity came in handy that day. The cascade of thoughts scared and surprised me. I was amazed at the quick contemplation to end my own life. I knew that without fear of the pain, I would have actually attempted. At 9, I didn't understand my own emotions, but I knew they weren't normal. So, I ran downstairs to tell my dad. I can only imagine the shock he felt hearing something like that. He then called my mom to share the news in a private conversation I didn't overhear.

I began counseling for a few months. I have vague memories of that time. A room full of toys, a pleasant middle-age woman. She asked me to draw pictures of myself and my family. "Here sweetie, why don't you play with these dolls." Unsure of what to do, I made them dance and play on the table. She followed up with what felt like a series of random pointless questions. I guess I provided the right answers because pretty soon after that, we all moved on. I don't remember talking about why I felt that way. About what led me to that moment. I am sure I was asked those very questions but had no clue how to explain it all. I was so shy and would retreat into my shell, brushing off what was too uncomfortable to express. I probably lied and said I didn't know what led me to that moment. It would have been easier. I did not have the words to express the sense of loss, longing and pain I was experiencing. At such a young age, I had a weird way of internalizing trauma and masking it well. I knew I had a lot to be grateful for. So I felt guilty at how deep the absence and inconsistencies of my mom hurt me. I felt I should be appreciative for what I had and get over everything else. Despite the difficulties I had a good life and great family. I was a competitive ice skater for years. In fact, it was my mom who put me in it. I practiced before and after school and won tons of competitions. I loved school. I had wonderful friends. I should be thankful. Why couldn't I shake the pain?

Let's go back a little further. Born on July 17, 1986, I was a true Cancer. Full of emotions that would rise and fall with the cycle of the moon. I've always had a hard shell that would protect a super soft interior. I was sensitive and sweet but would stick up for myself when necessary. Once as a small child I was at a local day care. It was a beautiful place, filled with wonderful people. The owner was Persian and there was a rainbow of children. In the living room stood a large grand piano. One I would happily bang on for hours. With no training I was completely out of key, but it was a great way to pass an afternoon. One particular day there was a little boy named John, who decided he was going to play with me. Despite the fact that I was perfectly happy to perform a solo. He hit a few keys as he slowly tried to nudge me out the way. I retaliated with a painful version of Twinkle Twinkle Little Star. He clanked back with own song. I fired back with a few random hits on my side of the piano. Rather quickly I grew tired of the competition and shoved him off the stool. I then returned to happily banging away until my parents arrived. They couldn't tell me until we got in the car, but both of my parents were proud of me. They always taught me to be kind and fair but stick up for myself as well. Although it very rarely came out, I think I got the aggressive part of my personality from my father. I was born to Kyle and Trisha Ickes. They had an inter-racial romance that resulted in a brief marriage and me. My dad was an intense, ex-military, guitar player, as well as a UC Berkeley graduate. As a young adult, he spent a few years in Madrid performing in flamenco shows. He played the guitar while his then-girlfriend danced. When he moved back to the States he performed in shows all over the Bay Area. He was a feature performer at big restaurants like the Spaghetti Factory in San Francisco. My dad was so handsome. Standing over 6 feet with fair skin, brown hair and light eyes, he never had an issue with the ladies. And he was always open to dating different races. His ex-girlfriends covered every race and shade. As was his nature, when he was committed to something, he was all in. It didn't matter if it was music, studies, a relationship or his child. When he focused on anything, you could count on him to take care of business 100%. He got the spirit of travel, exploring and liberalism from his family, yet in many ways, he rejected his roots. My father came from a well known, very prominent, very political family. My great-grandfather was Harold LeClair Ickes. He was Secretary of Interior for 13 years, becoming the longest person to ever hold that position to date. During his term, he was under President Franklin D Roosevelt. He was responsible for implementing much of his "New Deal." He was also head of the Public Works Administration. I was amazed to see he graced the July 1934 and the September 1941 cover of Time magazine. He had two sons. One was my grandfather Raymond, the other was my great uncle, Harold M. Ickes. Harold was famous for holding a position as chief of staff to President Clinton. He was also well known for fighting for civil rights. I later learned that he was beaten in a civil rights demonstration, fighting for the justice of people who looked nothing like him. He worked on the presidential campaign of many hopefuls, including Kennedy and Jesse Jackson. It's ironic that my father never once mentioned any of this. I started to learn about this aspect of my family history when seeing my great-grandfather's name in a history book in a 7th-grade class. The only reason it stood out was Ickes is such a unique name, one I was often teased for having. It's amazing how this source of embarrassment, one of the things that made me identifiably different during a time when I just wanted to fit in, later became a part of myself that I am most proud. During a time when I was struggling with feelings of rejection and worthlessness, seeing my family name in the history books created a small sense of pride. There is a power that comes from knowing your roots. One that could have served me well in my earlier years. I was proud of my family's accomplishments. There is something about knowing the strength of your ancestors, that imparts that same strength in you. You are more empowered to overcome your own struggles, when you witness others doing the same, especially when they are from your lineage. It could be learning the story of your grandmother who was physically abused but raised your mother with love. It could be witnessing the dedication and love of your father, who worked 15 hours a day to put you through college. It could be the strength of your mother, who gave you up for adoption, to give you all the opportunities she couldn't. In seeing the sacrifice, determination and strength of those who came before us- we are in turn more empowered for our own journey.

My grandfather was an interesting man. Raymond Wilmarth Ickes. By the time I was born he was much older. Our first pictures together are weathered, tucked in a box with an array of trinkets and memories. I was tiny, dressed in a little red Christmas outfit. He sat in a chair holding me, with a few sprouts of gray hair, a pair of glasses and a look of love. Quiet and unassuming, I never would have known his past. He was a retired lawyer and military vet. He earned his master's and law degree from the University of Chicago and in 1939 became a prosecutor for federal crimes. He was outspoken and directly involved in ending Japanese internment in the United States. He was also a prosecutor in the Nuremberg Trials in Germany. He was actually on Richard Nixon's enemy list. These things were fascinating because my memories of him were quiet and peaceful. I don't remember us ever having much conversation although I visited him and his wife, Janet, regularly growing up. They lived 5 minutes from my father and I in a huge home in the Berkeley hills. I was surprised to learn as an adult that he received a purple heart and a silver star while serving in the Marines, after being injured in Iwo Jima. These things were never discussed, at least not with me. I discovered it after receiving a call from a stranger, saying that my grandfather saved his father's life. I was in my 30s. It sent me down a rabbit hole of google searches and inquisitive calls to my father. While my father was unimpressed, these were things I found so intriguing.

Grandpa Raymond's house was huge. A gorgeous three-story home in the Berkeley hills. It was a wooden building with a commanding presence. There were large rooms and grand windows. When you walk into the first floor, your eyes are immediately drawn to the high ceilings, which make the house feel even more massive. The next thing you can't help but notice is a huge staircase. On the banister, there was literally a skinned tiger. I kid you not; this tiger sat draped over the staircase. Two legs and gigantic paws dangled on each side of the rail. Enthralled with its huge teeth and large head, I remember gingerly rubbing a canine before running upstairs as some sort of weird ritual every time I came over. I don't remember listening to music or watching television, but I was always entertained. Without any of that, it was still absolutely fascinating. The house was full of unique objects. And although I don't remember any signs of politics, war or medals, they were probably there. What I do remember, what I spent hours gazing at, were pieces of another part of his life. He was liberal with a profound sense of righteousness. Since a young child, he was very interested in Native American culture. He spoke both Ojibwa and Navajo. I mean, how many people do you know that speak 2 Native American languages? He also spent a year living with the Ojibwa tribe. As a child, I loved seeing moccasins, bowls and other unique treasures from that time in his life. Beautiful beaded jewelry sat on display in a clear case. I would sit next to it for hours, staring at all its beautiful contents. His home, along with my love of reading, sparked an early interest in different cultures, people and ways of life. Walking through his house made me realize how much of the world there was to see and discover.

My experience of a grandmother (on my dad's side) was Janet Ickes. She taught me how to knit. We spent hours practicing the knit and rib stitch. I came back to my dad proudly displaying the blankets and scarves we made. She took me shopping and made me waffles with strawberry jam. Their house had a big backyard that led directly to a trail in the hills. We would often take their 3 dogs for long walks, exploring nature and eating blueberries off random bushes. Hiking until I was too tired, before heading back home. We had a good relationship growing up, but she and my father were pretty distant. She was a pleasant stepmother, but I think he always missed his mom. She passed away from cancer when my dad was in his 20s. Miralotte was an amazing woman I wish I had a chance to meet or even to learn more about before adulthood. As a child I gazed at her picture for hours. It hung in my room and I was mesmerized by her beauty, both inside and out. My dad told me how she would cross out n**ger in every book she read to them. The word was banned from her house, despite being normal in her surroundings. As an adult I learned she was the statewide rifle champion. She was well known as one of the most iconic women in high power rifle shooting history. Once I researched, there were tons of articles and pictures of her online. She made a name for herself. Her father, Dr. Louis W. Sauer, was a famous pediatrician who perfected the vaccine for preventing whooping cough in 1931. At that time, it was a leading cause of death in children under the age of 2. He eventually created the DTap vaccine. He changed millions of lives and never asked for a penny. He was on record as stating, "One does not do these types of things for money." The more I learned about my family history, the more I was inspired and wanted to make an impact. Every new piece of information deposited a little seed inside of me that would produce fruit many years later. It was amazing to see this theme of philanthropy and high character. I was so proud to see that the white side of my family consistently stood up against a system that benefited them. They were rich, white, in government and yet constantly fighting for civil rights and other liberties. Whether it was advancement in medicine, being pioneers in their field or fighting for civil rights, my family history made me proud. Knowing even a little of this growing up could have greatly altered my sense of self-worth as a child.

Learning my mother's side of the family was very different. Where I could google anyone on my dad's side, alternatively my mother's side I experienced. Although the majority of my time was spent with my dad growing up, he and my maternal grandmother made sure I saw that side of the family often. My granny is a traditional African American southern woman. She was the daughter of a postal worker and a housewife. Her mother went back to work when she was old enough to start school. She was the baby of 5 children, one of whom died at birth. My grandmother shared stories of visiting her own grandmother during the summers. Her grandmother lived in the country, didn't know how to read or write, but could cook up a storm. She witnessed her go to the backyard to hand pick the eggs for the mornings and the live chicken for that evening's dinner. I cringed as she described the animal's last moments. They would chase the chicken through the yard, pick it up by the neck and swing it round and round in circles. Swish, swish, swish. Eventually the head would separate from the body, sending the poor animal flying. It would then continue to run around the backyard headless, until it finally dropped. Then the kids would run out through the grass barefoot, scoop it up and bring it inside. As a group they pulled and tugged at the feathers, plucking every last one out the body. Once the chicken was clean and ready to be cooked, my grandma would run off to play. She loved those summers. It was a different experience than the city life she normally lived. She came from a family that instilled the importance of church, education, strong values and hard work. All siblings except one, graduated college. Growing up with Mary Logan meant lie was a curse word and you better not ever set your lips to be disrespectful. If you were telling the story of someone who spoke a mistruth, you knew to say they told a story. My grandmother instilled a love of food, travel and church in us all. Every Sunday, we smelled yams, greens, oxtails, chicken, black-eyed peas, rice and some sort of yummy dessert. She is a deeply religious, church-going AKA straight out of Monroe, Louisiana. She spent her entire life as an educator and created a love of learning in us all. She began to teach us to read at 3 years old. She moved to the Bay Area with my grandfather, Frank Logan, in the 50s, when my mother and aunt were very young. She was a teacher and later a principal, who always commanded poise and integrity. Her words of wisdom stayed in my mind throughout my whole life, even when I didn't follow them. To whom much is given, much is required. Your character is who you are when no one is looking, as well as loads of bible verses I still know by heart. My cousins and I started reciting the Lord's Prayer early and were so proud when we had it memorized. We were a part of everything you could think of at our small church. We were acolytes, which essentially means you light candles in the beginning of church service and put them out at the end. We remained in that position for years despite dropping the candles one Sunday, knocking over a basket of small papers and proceeding to set a little portion of the church on fire. We were mortified as we stood helpless in front of the church, looking on while the blaze was stomped out by several ladies in large hats. If only our embarrassment was as easily extinguished. We sang in the children's choir. It didn't matter that my voice cracked every other note. They just needed bodies in the pew and my grandma was happy to oblige with her three granddaughters. At least I learned how to do a mean lip sync. We attended Sunday school and later taught it. During the summers we attended Daily Vacation Bible study, which was a church summer camp. We stood in front of the church to recite poems, and we fixed food for the homeless on holidays. One year, my three cousins and I were cracking what seemed like an endless stream of eggs to prepare for breakfast at the shelter. The adults were seasoning and scrambling away. The whole room smelled yummy, and I was having a great time. My younger cousin Kia had gone to lay out the utensils and serve the guests. When she came back in the kitchen, something was off. Even as a child, I was very sensitive to other's emotions. As an empath, it was deeper than caring about an individual. I actually felt other's emotions as if they were my own. So, when she walked back in the room, I was overcome with shock and sadness but didn't know why. I asked her what happened and she shared that a girl from her class was at one of the tables waiting to be served. She was in shock and so sad for the little girl. She shared how the classmate stared down at the table, refusing to make eye contact. We told her we would serve the food instead, in order to save the girl further embarrassment. Kia promised not to tell a soul about the little girl's secret. It was an astounding wake-up call to us all. It imparted a lesson deep inside of me that never left, you never know what another person is going through, and at all times, you must be kind. Now was I always kind, of course not. But I truly tried. It also made me very aware that as much as I struggled in my own life, things could always be ten times worse. I didn't like that my mom lived in motels, but at least she wasn't in a shelter or on the street. Plus, I always had my dad's house. I learned to thank God that day for what I did have. If we search, we can always find a piece of good in almost every situation. As I stood in the kitchen, counting my blessings, I felt so grateful. I thought to myself, in actuality, my mom had been in one motel so long it became like home. We knew the other people who lived there. Several rooms housed families or couples. I was not the only child, despite sticking to myself. I learned hotels are for getaways. Motels become homes. The owners were kind. They even had a daughter around my age. As I got older, one of the owners used to bring me back clothes and treats when he returned from visiting his home country Pakistan. I was not shuffled around or unsure of where I would be the next evening. While the lack of privacy really bothered me, at least it was only a lack of privacy from my mom, not from a ton of strangers. God showed me that day to always be grateful, that even when things aren't ideal, there is someone out there who would appreciate what you have.

Looking back, I am so thankful for the collaboration between my father and my maternal grandparents. I was born in the 80s, and even for the time period my dad's apartment was in some ways like a blast from the past. To this day, his apartment has an original rotary phone and a gas pilot stove. This meant long dials and lighting the oven with a match. That didn't restrict my phone conversations, but it did limit how much cooking was done. Once I was trying to figure out how to work the stove and was so confused. I had turned on the gas and spent far too long trying to figure out how to light it. By the time the match was lit, it sparked a huge flame that singed the hair on my hands and sealed the deal on me ever trying to use the oven again. From there on, the top of the stove would have to do. Thankfully when I was a kid, my dad was great at making burgers (despite being a vegetarian), grilled cheese sandwiches, bowls of cereal and scooping our favorite treat, ice cream. Still, grandma's house took cooking and eating to a whole new level and I loved it. Saturday morning breakfasts were eggs, bacon, biscuits, French toast and sausage patties. Lunch could be burgers, pizza or spaghetti. Big dinners were saved for Sundays. Ox tails, barbequed chicken, potato salad, yams, mac and cheese and salad. My stomach was always happy. But my favorite part of going over there was playing hours with my cousins Noel and Kia. Noel was the sister I never had. We were born 5 days apart and she was a built in best friend. She lived in Los Angeles for a long time. My favorite part of the summers was riding to the airport to pick her up. We had big imaginations and were super creative. At one point we were convinced we could build our own car. That never got out the planning stage. When we gave up on that we planned on constructing a clubhouse in the backyard. We eventually settled on a spare room downstairs. We stayed up late watching movies that would scar us for life. The original version of It was traumatizing to us all. I still think that movie should be banned. It took years before we would go in the bathroom alone, always afraid a clown would somehow come out the drain. We spent hours making up dances to MC Hammer and Salt-N-Pepa. We played out The Boy is Mine. She was Brandy and I was Monica. We created the NNK club and put on shows in my grandma's backyard, ones we had the nerve to actually charge for. We created tickets, itineraries and spent time setting up a stage. We had fun expressing our creativity and the adults obliged. To top it off I got the cutest hairstyles by my auntie Janelle. Braids and ponytails to last me for the week. That was a great bonus because on the one hand my dad was the one to buy my first pads and feminine hygiene products. I could talk to him about anything. On the other hand, my dad is a white ex-military man's man, and attempting to tame my hair wasn't realistic. I had hair like a lion. It was big, free and wild unless my aunt gave me a style to last hold me over. Usually, I went to school with tangled, messy hair. It defied gravity, floating in whichever direction it chose. My dad's version of doing my hair consisted of putting a headband on it, maybe with an added barrette if we were really feeling fancy. Eventually, a black teacher at my elementary school, who also went to church with my grandma, decided enough was enough and began doing my hair regularly during lunch. I loved Ms.Woolbright so much, and my little hairstyles were extra cute. She took me under her wing. Pretty soon, girls of all races were lining up for ponytail styles with beads and knocker balls. She would gently say "You have to ask your mom baby." before looking at me with a smile. Every now and then a mother would agree and I would have matching hair styles with a little blonde classmate.

Now the other favorite part of my grandma's house was my grandpa. My mother and I were his favorites and he did not try to hide that fact. I always felt so special with him. I would go in his room and happily climb in his bed. I didn't mind that it was covered in newspapers and random items. I didn't even need to get under the covers. He spent hours watching shows like the Jeffersons and Soul Train and I was just happy to snuggle up with him. We ate boxes of vanilla wafers and I was in heaven because time with him was the best. He was so gentle and kind, I could lay with him for hours. He never got tired of asking me, "Who you love the best?" and I would shyly reply, "I love you, Grandpa." which made him fall out in the biggest laughter. Once I wanted this special outfit and I happened to mention it to him. The next morning there was an envelope with my name on it. Inside was $100. Double enough to cover the outfit. I was surrounded by love. It was experienced and felt. Yet something about human nature makes us yearn so deeply for that bond and connection with our parents. Despite the amazing network of family I had around me, nothing could take away the sting of not being a priority to my own mother. It is something I wrestled with for a long time. For years I was trying to mask the pain of a little girl who never felt like she was enough. The thing about ignoring sadness and pain is that eventually, it turns into anger. And anyone walking around sad and angry is a danger to themselves or someone else.

When shifts and transitions shake you to
the core, see that as a sign of the greatness
that's going to occur.

-Chelsea Dinen

Chapter 2- Transitions

Middle school is hard for a lot of children. For me, it was the beginning of a series of events that would change the course of my life. I was already struggling, but these years were particularly difficult and agonizing. However, like all struggles, it was designed to push me to exactly where I was meant to go. Of course there were some parts I enjoyed. My mom always wanted me to be in a sport. As a young child she chose ballet, which I did until the 3rd grade. I enjoyed the recitals. But rehearsals were painfully boring and I begged my dad to take me out. Since he was the one taking me to practice, and hearing my daily complaints, eventually he obliged. Shortly after that I began ice skating. I loved it. The freedom of gliding down the ice. Spinning and jumping, defying gravity. Swaying to the music, in my own world. The commitment was a lot but well worth it. I practiced at 6am and again right after school. I ran for endurance and took stretching classes for flexibility. I competed in local competitions, winning several. When preparing for my first routine, my coach told me to pick music I would like to skate to. I spent all day with my dad, pouring through different Janet Jackson albums. I finally settled on Control. I envisioned my outfit, convinced we could incorporate a leather vest. If I was lucky maybe I would even get to wear the famous one glove. At my next practice I was excited to tell my coach my choice. She smiled and told me that wouldn't work. I ended up skating to a classical piece she picked out. I was aware of the cultural differences, but despite my disappointment I still enjoyed it. As I got older my attention began to drift and ice skating became more of a commitment than I wanted to make. After several years I decided to quit. Again, my dad was fine with whatever I wanted. Until 14, I lived primarily with my father. He was fiercely protective and equally overbearing. He wasn't perfect, but he loved me and was there for me in ways no one would ever match. He would play endless board games with me as a child, letting me win every time. He never tired of Parcheesi, cooking for me, making my bed or letting me talk about whatever was on my mind. He was the parent that always had my back. Physically, emotionally and financially, he was always there. Old classmates still laugh at the time he chased my teacher through the halls with my brother on his shoulders for giving me a B when I deserved an A. He didn't break out into a full run, but his brisk walk and aggressive energy kept my teacher motivated enough to stay several steps in front of him. After that incident, any meetings with my dad and a teacher were always held in the principal's office with a security guard present. It was a bit over the top, but the way he supported me was appreciated. There are some areas that even my dad will admit he was a bit excessive. Everything we owned was in bulk. We always had 10 boxes of the exact same cereal. Freezer full of the same three items. Countless rolls of tissue and paper towels. We never ever ran out of anything. Food outside of the kitchen was a bit of a production. When I would eat lunch in my room, I always sat on the floor on top of this beautiful multi-colored rug so I wouldn't get crumbs in my bed. It was a perfect setup because it was right in front of my TV where I would watch my favorite shows Sister Sister, Full House and 7th Heaven. Watching Boy Meets World convinced me I would meet the love of my life at 12. I would eat, laugh and enjoy myself. Ignoring the fact that if I glanced up, I would see my dad peeking in the room, waiting for the exact moment I finished my plate. If I had to use the bathroom, I learned to announce, "Please don't take the plate, I am still eating." It was a lesson learned the hard way after several times of leaving my food momentarily unguarded. Only to walk back in the room, confused as to where my food went. Discovering upon further inspection that my plate was whisked away and the dishes were washed during the five minutes I had stepped out. At whatever point I was done eating, he would then come back in and vacuum the rug. After that, he mopped the hardwood floor surrounding it. Every single time. While I appreciate a clean house like anyone else, the rigidity and over-attention to detail was stressful and irritating.

There also seemed to be an overlying level of anxiety at all times. My dad would frantically cover my eyes at every commercial he found the least bit inappropriate. He would run over to me, panic-stricken at any possibility of danger. This could be anything from tripping over the curb, hitting my head on a passing branch or stumbling and scraping a knee. The level of overreaction, although coming from a good place, was taxing. Once my father, stepmother, and I were going to a wedding in San Francisco. It was tense because, as usual, my dad was rushing us to get out of the house. "We have to drive, park and walk over. We can't be late!" We literally heard different versions of that all morning. My stepmother Lauren kept assuring him we had time, but he was frantic with worry we may end up running behind. Eventually, we all piled in the car and made the 25-minute drive into the city. We lucked out and found great parking. We hopped out of the car and huddled together as the wind pushed us rather forcefully down the street. We swung open the doors to the church, all relieved that we had made it and stood there confused. We didn't recognize anyone, not even the bride and groom. We had arrived during the previous wedding of the day. It could have been a laughable moment, but after the tension, arguing and yelling all morning, to arrive hours early was not funny. Little incidents like this weren't a big deal, but the constant rushing, rigidity and pressure were overwhelming. It was not uncommon to get over 10–15 pages from my dad in a day. This was before the time of cell phones when you kept a beeper on your hip and would see a tiny number cross the screen any time someone needed to reach you. By middle school, I had hormones and emotions raging and was no longer the shy, quiet girl I used to be. We were both constantly frustrated, yelling and angry. I would vent in my diary only to be confronted by its contents after my dad read all my deepest thoughts. I felt smothered and like my privacy was betrayed. Once it escalated to where he spit in my face. It was during one of our many screaming matches. He felt I was out of control. I had stolen clothes from a local store, which is obviously horrendous behavior. I'm sure I said things I shouldn't have, and my dad lost control and slung a huge glob of spit directly in my face. The level of rage I felt was unmatched. I contemplated grabbing a knife to defend myself and instead spat right back. I made an internal promise that would never happen again. I ended up on the phone with my maternal grandmother, who told me to pack my things and move in with her. I have always admired her so much, so I was happy for the option. I moved in with her right before the beginning of my 9th-grade year.

I spent a year living in Richmond with my grandma, aunt and two cousins Noel and Kia. It didn't work out long term for a variety of reasons. The main because I was in a rebellious stage. Coming from my dad's, I was simply tired of having my every move regulated. At this point, I was in high school, thought I was "grown" and liked to smoke weed and party. Now don't get me wrong I was smart. I was in honors and AP classes, but my heart and mind were drifting away from school. I was over it and just wanted to have fun. Half the time I would skip school, head to San Francisco and go shoplifting. Knowing stealing was wrong but enjoying the thrill. Leaving Nordstroms with $200 jeans I didn't need and couldn't afford. Testing the limits to see what I would get away with. Pushing my guilt to the back of my mind. I would show up to school on test days only, doing the bare minimum to pass. After school, I wanted to go with friends and hang out and party. I was on a path that was not ok with my grandmother. She was not one for parties and things like that, but I knew how to manipulate the situation. I would call my mom at work to ask for her permission, knowing she would say yes. The only difficult part was getting her to answer the phone. During one conversation I was angry at how difficult it was for me to reach her. She told me going forward I could do whatever I want and did not have to ask for her consent. However, the only caveat was that I also wasn't to call her if I needed help or got in trouble. A little piece of me was hurt. There's that dichotomy again. I wanted to go hang out, but I also wanted her to care. I wanted to run wild, but I also wanted it to matter to my mom where I went and what I did. I wanted her to ask who my friends were and what we were doing. Instead, I took that statement and ran with it. I was hanging out at parties and with friends whenever I felt like it. I was living out of alignment with my morals. Looking back, I should have listened to my grandmother and stayed home.

An added piece of the puzzle was how alone I felt in that house after my grandpa passed away. When he died, I was devastated. He worked as a car valet well into his 70s. The rule was that if the gate was up, the employees were to drive the cars into the elevator. It would then lift them to various floors to park. One afternoon the gate was raised up and he slowly drove in. As he pulled into the elevator, he immediately knew something was wrong. The front wheels dropped down, followed by the nose of the car. He slammed on the brakes but it was too late to stop. He plunged down several stories without wearing a seat belt. It was amazing that he survived, but it wasn't without issues. Even before this incident, he was suffering from a lot of pain and overall poor health. After the accident his body was overwhelmed. He limped around the house groaning, always in pain. He needed surgery but his heart wasn't strong. His doctor told him without the surgery he would be a quadriplegic. He was battling heart issues, high blood pressure and diabetes. All that before his accident. The surgeon explained he may not be strong enough to survive surgery. He looked my grandmother in the eyes "Baby, I have to take that risk." He walked into the hospital for surgery a few months later and never walked back out. He knew it was his time. Frank Logan told my grandmother he would not be coming back home. He left all of his affairs in order and left an envelope for my grandmother to open after he passed. I can't imagine how that made her feel. To lose the man she loved. The man she met on her summer break from college. They met in June and married secretly by August. He was the father of her children and the man she stayed with until the day he died. He was all she had ever truly known. For me, it was devastating. I loved him with my whole being. Shortly after his death is when I first realized just how different I was. I had an experience I hadn't had before and have not had since. After the funeral, everyone was at my grandma's house eating good food, exchanging beautiful stories and sharing fun memories. I was walking down the hall into the kitchen, when I looked over to my right and stopped in my tracks. There he was. Standing at the bottom of the stairs, his right foot resting on the stair above the left. Leaning slightly to the right, clutching on the banister for support, as if he was out of breath. He looked completely normal, yet it was also the craziest thing I had ever witnessed. I was so confused. I knew my grandfather could not be there, yet I was looking right at him. He wasn't translucent like I had always seen in the movies.

He wasn't gliding across the floor like I thought ghosts did. He looked every bit as real as he did when he was alive. So clearly there that I had no doubt in my mind what I was seeing. My heart was beating fast and I felt flushed, so I ran into the kitchen. I stood there for about a minute, mind racing. No one noticed me, so I crept back to the top of the stairs and looked again, but he was gone. To this day, I wish I had sat longer or tried to talk to him. As I stepped back into the kitchen a second time, I suppose I looked so frightened someone asked me what was wrong. I can't even remember who it was, but I immediately shared my experience. When I told my grandmother, she was quick to tell me that as much as she loved him, she didn't need any visits and would happily wait to see him on the other side. To fully understand this statement, you had to know my grandpa. He wasn't much of a talker. He would sit for hours reading a newspaper or watching T.V., picking and choosing when he responds to you. I'm guessing she felt like the time to get chatty, wasn't after his death.

I've looked into this a lot and I believe our souls don't always leave directly after death. Often, they take some time to fully transition to the other side. When I say the other side, I am referring to heaven, reincarnation or whatever it is that comes next. I think often there is a transition period. A time where the body has passed away, but the spirit is hanging around. The amount of time the spirit stays on this physical plane depends on how the individual died and where they were mentally and emotionally when it happened. In my opinion, when death is unexpected or a shock, it may take longer for the soul to come to terms with what has happened and be ready to leave. I also believe that quite often, people stay around to check in on loved ones and family. Now what happens after the soul is ready to cross over is a bit of a mystery to me. I often wonder about what happens next. I don't believe in hell in the sense of a devil with a pitchfork, poking at souls condemned to an eternity in flames. I believe there is some form of a heaven you stay in until you are reincarnated. And my belief is that hell is probably a nothingness. Being eternally stuck between. I suppose that's why I have never been drawn to visiting a grave. I understand and respect why that has a lot of meaning for so many people. I also completely agree with people grieving in whatever way they need to. But due to my belief that the soul leaves the body directly after its passing, I find other ways to create solace for myself. For my grandpa, I fully trust that he ended up in heaven, but it took a while. Maybe because I was his favorite, maybe because I was in tune in a unique way, he made his presence known for many years after his passing. Sometimes, I would be writing or watching TV and I could literally feel his presence come into the room. My dog would growl, bark and eventually run to hide under my bed. It never scared me, though. It is very similar to being out and feeling someone staring at you, only to glance up and lock eyes with someone. Only this time I didn't have the visual confirmation. It's not a negative feeling, it's just odd. Actually, as crazy as it may sound, it was quite comforting and I missed it when he was gone. I went back to feeling alone, but that was after many years of him showing he was still around. At times there was physical contact which other people were a witness to. It was quite a relief because I doubt anyone truly believed me until they experienced it for themselves. For example, there was one occasion when my cousin Monica was spending the night. She was lying on the couch in the living room.

"Cousin!"

I got out of my bed and came into the room. "What's up?"

"Did you just do that?" she asked.

"Huh?"

Apparently, the light had popped on out of nowhere. I laughed and told her it was my grandpa because at the time, things like that were totally normal around me. Her eyes got wide and her breathing changed. She was considerably less amused and told me she wouldn't be coming back to my house. Another incident was with my other cousin Noel. We were downstairs at my grandma's house listening to music. All of a sudden, the volume shot up on the radio. Seeing as though we were on the floor chatting and nowhere near the remote, we looked at each other surprised. I bent my head slightly towards her and halfway joking said, "Don't worry, it's just my ghost." The moment those words left my lips, and I do mean the exact moment, the volume shot up to its max. We looked at each other, screamed and ran upstairs as fast as we could. Although I knew it was him, the shock caught us both off guard. Things like that continued to happen over the next few years, some with witnesses, many more in private. A television randomly turning on or keys disappearing for hours, only to reappear in a place I had looked countless times. Ghosts can affect electrical currents. Researchers have found elevated magnetic fields in areas that are believed to be haunted. One night when I was about 15, I developed an elaborate plan to sneak out of my grandma's house. I had a good friend Tiffani over, but a boy I liked was coming outside to sit and talk with me. The issue was how to get out of the house undetected. There were 5 doors leading in and out of my grandmother's house. Three of those doors were downstairs and since my aunt and cousins' rooms were downstairs, I didn't even want to attempt that. One of the upstairs doors was inside my grandmother's room, so that obviously wasn't going to work. I also knew I couldn't go out of the front door because it was right next to my grandma's room. So that left the one door that wasn't near any sleeping adult. I decided to sneak out of the door in the kitchen. The only issue was if you walk across the kitchen floor, it creaks so loud my aunt was sure to hear, especially because she was a notoriously light sleeper. I had a plan though. I told Tiffani I was going outside for 30 minutes or less. I got up and crept down the hall past my first checkpoint, my grandma's room. Once I passed that safely I made a right and crossed the carpeted (and silent) living and dining room. Now was the tricky part, getting through the kitchen silently. I hopped on the counter and scooted to the end, cautiously avoiding pots, pans and anything that makes noise. I slowly opened the door and was about to walk out when a bang scared the hell out of me. There's a door that separates the two upstairs bedrooms from the rest of the top floor. This is the door that slammed extremely loud at 2 AM. At this point, my heart is pounding. I'm not sure if I called Tiffani or if she called me, but we were both scared and you could hear the panic in her voice.

"Did you just slam the door???" she forced out in a terrified whisper.

"Of course not!" At this point, I was literally almost out of the house. "Check to see if it was my grandma, please!"

She peeked and reported it wasn't. Then I knew what was going on. He didn't like me sneaking out.

"I'm scared!" she whispered.

"Get up and come out with me."

She stayed in bed, probably scared to death. To this day that makes me chuckle. My grandpa was always looking out for me, even beyond the grave.

By the time I was 15, I was smoking weed daily and drinking occasionally. Weed was my crutch and alcohol was an occasional addition. In many ways, being high removed me as a fully active participant in life and sidelined me as an observer. I was experiencing life through a filter. My emotions slightly dulled, protected with a blanket of insensitivity that was a welcome relief. One that protected me for years. Big stuff became little stuff and the little stuff didn't matter. I was partially numb pretty much all of the time. Viewing the world through a hazy curtain. Desperately stuffing down old memories, masking old wounds and pushing through life, pretending everything was fine. There were times I would wake up in the middle of the night mind racing, only to sneak outside with a partially rolled blunt so I could doze back off to sleep. When I was clear, my mind was flooded with the things I hadn't worked through. The things I simply wanted to forget. Of course, now I understand that you have to work through what you've gone through. You can't stuff down pain, regrets and trauma because it will all eventually surface. However, for a long time, I was oblivious and stuck in the mental trap of victimhood. Why me, instead of how do I overcome this, was my go-to attitude. So, every time I was sober, and sometimes when I wasn't, memories would rise to the surface like a ball being stuffed under water. Held down temporarily but breaking forcefully through the surface every time I let down my guard. Faint echoes and torments, growing louder the more I resisted. Recollections I hoped would disappear. Years had passed, situations had transpired, but inside I was the same little girl. Only now with a storm of emotions and experiences raging inside of me. I think it was a little too much for my grandmother, understandably so. I had a lot of work to do, which I was avoiding. By the 10th grade I moved out to try living with my mom and Kenny.

I was hesitant but excited to be living with my mom, full time, for the first time since I was 3. We were in a beautiful little apartment I helped her find. It was her first time out of a motel since I was a toddler. All the rooms were almost completely empty except for mine. Bare of furniture, pictures or anything that would normally make it feel like home. So, when I came home, I always belted straight to my room. I had a bed from Ikea whose slabs were always falling apart and needing to be arranged. My entertainment was a TV that stood on top of several blue milk crates, covered with a sheet I found buried in my closet. This is where perspective comes into play. Despite things not being ideal, I absolutely loved having my own space. It was my sanctuary. I would vent in my diary, write poetry and spend hours by myself. I loved the privacy and space. It was in this room I tried ecstasy for the first time. My boyfriend Kevin handed me a pill. Being young, in love and overly trusting, I took it without even asking what it was. That is insane. You should never ingest or try an unknown substance. I look back surprised at my own foolishness. However, at first, it was the best thing ever. It made me happy, excited and I felt like I was on top of the world. I had no worries, no hurt and no pain. It gave me energy and the feeling I could accomplish anything. Kevin and I laughed and talked for hours. Some days we would catch the bus and BART, exploring the city. Ecstasy is a mood enhancer and we were young, in love and having fun. But like any drug, it was a slippery slope. I lost control. Relatively quickly I was taking it every day. I got addicted to how good it made me feel. There was no desire to go back to constant tears, over emotions and repetitive thoughts. Pretty soon, I decided high school was no longer for me and convinced my parents to sign me out. It wasn't their first choice but I had made up my mind. Kevin and I began to spend almost every waking moment together. He was living undetected at my mom's house for months. Despite sharing a wall with my mom, we tried to be as quiet as possible. On the rare occasions when my mom came into my room he hid in the closet. We began to develop an unhealthy attachment exacerbated by drugs, sex and a lot of fights. The drugs caused the mood to shift in the blink of an eye. Things could quickly change from happy to dangerous. The first time he hit me, we were in my room at my mom's apartment. I have no idea what we were arguing about but all of a sudden, his hand connected to the side of my face. He wasn't a small guy and I crumpled to the floor in pain, scared to fight back. It hurt physically, but the true pain went much deeper. I really loved him and I just couldn't believe he would put his hands on me. I learned quickly because after the first time it kept happening. I no longer laid there. We have to be careful what lines we cross. Once certain lines are stepped over, it is so much easier to cross them again. After that first fight, I was quick to fight back. If I even thought he was going to hit me, I attacked first. He left bruises on me and once I busted his nose. When I saw the blood I took off running, terrified at what he might do. We argued outside in the middle of the street. He would toss me into the bushes but I would hop back up and attack. I know we looked crazy as hell. But for some reason we kept hanging on. Eventually we got tired of sneaking around my mom's. So, for almost 6 months we moved in with Kevin's father. It was fun at first. We were playing house and there were no rules. His father was so sweet and would come to my defense when we argued. But Kevin was so angry he threatened him when he tried to intervene. His dad came out as gay when Kevin was 13. His dad's husband was someone he originally thought was a roommate. It wasn't until they moved across the country together from D.C. to Cali, that he realized it must be something more. Out of the two, his dad was more feminine, which bothered Kevin a lot. Because of that he was mean and aggressive towards him. As much as he wanted to, there was nothing his father could do to help. So he sat back and stayed out of it, even when we were out of control. Kevin wasn't only wild with me. He was also selling drugs. Eventually, he got into legal trouble and was sent to the East Coast to live with his mom in hopes he would calm down. I moved back into my mom's. A month after he left, I found out I was pregnant with a baby I could not keep.

Lord, if I could go back, I would tell my younger self, baby, you've got to grow through what you go through. Learn the lessons! Get better! Be strong! But I was still in victim mode, and because of that, I was angry. I have since learned that anger is only unprocessed pain. It is sadness and hurt we have not yet worked through. I had so much I still needed to let go of. I had not yet learned that pain is the catalyst for success. It is the preparation for our future. By this point, so much had changed since that day in my dad's kitchen. Yet somehow, so much was the same. I spent years stuck in the same place emotionally. Rooted in pain, unable to break the chains of my self-imposed misery. I still felt worthless. Desperately unhappy. Too young, immature and unaware to grasp that happiness is a decision. A choice I had yet to make. I was exhausted and sick from riding the roller coaster of my own emotions. So, one day about a year after Kevin left, I decided I was done. I was deeply spiritual and imagined the peace of going with God and my grandfather would have to be much better than being here. Not that I ever truly wanted to die; it was that I could not fathom continuing the way I had been going. Living in chronic depression was something I could no longer do. From my very limited perspective, death seemed the only way out. From my previous experience, which I couldn't even call a true attempt, I knew that slitting my wrist was out of the question. Despite years of broken promises to myself, I kept the one I made that day at 9 years old. If I ever truly attempted suicide, I would do it in the gentlest way possible. Hanging seemed horrific. A gun was too violent, a knife too much pain. As I looked around, I realized I had a bottle of sleeping pills. In my warped mind, it all made perfect sense. Once I decided, there was a gush of relief followed by an equally intense wave of sadness. I cried and cried until my eyes were swollen. I ripped a blank piece of paper out of my diary and scribbled everything that came to mind. I wish I could say it was loving, honest and self-accountable, but it wasn't. It was angry. Mostly at my mom. I remember distinctly wanting her to be the one to find my body. The truth is I was angry towards myself. But that's the part I wasn't ready to admit yet. It is much easier to blame outside people, events and circumstances than to hold yourself accountable. It is difficult to take accountability for the life you have created, but that is the only way to grow. Unfortunately, I wasn't there yet. After rambling for 2 pages, I grabbed the bottle and shook out the last 6 pills. Deep down, I knew it wouldn't be enough to kill me. I don't know if I just wanted to sleep for a very long time or if I never wanted to wake up. What I was desperate for was peace. At that moment, I saw this as the only way to achieve that, so I took them all. I laid back to get comfortable for whatever was next and sent a goodbye text to my new boyfriend. Unknowingly he stopped what he was doing and drove like a bat out of hell to my house. I heard footsteps pounding up the steps to our second-story apartment. Then loud banging at the door.

The next few hours are pretty foggy in my memory. I remember certain pieces. My mom screamed hysterically, "The advice nurse said you can't go to sleep."

I wasn't moved. "She said you won't wake up." I responded with a blank stare. My bed was so warm and comfortable. I thought to myself, if this works, I picked the right way to go. My mom and boyfriend wanted me to go to Kaiser, and at first, I resisted. After hours of crying and months of contemplating, I had finally made a feeble attempt at silencing the pain. The hospital was the last place I wanted to go. I was presented with the option of them calling the ambulance or going willingly in the car. I pictured a struggle and the paramedics storming our apartment. I imagined them strapping me to a gurney and carrying me to the ambulance. The neighbors peeking through peepholes and barely parted curtains. My face red, full of tears, angry, sad and embarrassed. Never one for a scene, I chose the car. My mom drove me to the Kaiser close to our house. When I climbed in the back seat, I felt good. Nice and relaxed, completely unconcerned about whether my plan would actually work. Life, death, it didn't matter now. My head rested against the glass, the blur of dark buildings and bright lights as we sped down the street. The window was down and I felt a cool breeze on my face. Was this heaven? Definitely not, but it did feel good. That was short-lived. Pretty soon we pulled up to the hospital, and almost immediately, the nausea took over. I threw up outside the car window the moment the car stopped and again once we got inside the emergency room. I struggled to answer what felt like endless questions. I was too embarrassed to look the nurse in the eye. Even in that moment, I was more concerned about what people would think about me than if I would be ok. I didn't want to admit to a stranger that I tried to kill myself, and barely at that. Six pills are a joke. They gave me charcoal to drink, and then I went into the waiting room restroom to throw up several times. They told me if I couldn't throw it up, they would have to pump my stomach. I've always had the strangest phobia of throwing up. It's admittedly overdramatic. Grabbing the sink as I am choking, crying, praying and gasping for air. I was miserable. Glancing back and forth from the sink to the white tile, stomach doing flips waiting for the next round. Everything creeping back up the way it went down. Disgusted with myself as I heaved and regurgitated all I could. My throat was on fire. My eyes were burning, my body was tired and my mind was numb. Eventually, they got me into a room where I was finally able to curl up in a ball and to go to sleep.

Several hours later, my eyes slowly opened. For a moment, I was confused and forgot where I was and why. I looked up and noticed a security guard outside my room. He's handsome, I thought to myself. He was a young man, maybe in his 20s. Tall, built and chocolate with a beard. He glanced up at me occasionally before looking back down at his clipboard. Hmm, that's odd. I wonder why he's sitting there, must be on a break or something. I asked my parents, who were both there by then, what was going on, and they informed me that I was on a 51/50 suicide hold and watch. My face instantly got hot as I realized the security guard was there for me. Even though he was just doing his job, I felt humiliated. I just wanted him to go away. I wanted to go home to escape the curious looks and endless questions. I was relieved my attempt didn't work. It sounds so strange to say, but that quick I thought I was over it. While laying in the hospital bed, I was ready to put this incident in a box and tuck it into the back of my memories. Like I said, my emotions were a roller coaster. I had halfway tried, fully failed and was totally ready to move on like nothing happened. But it was too late for that. Now Kaiser was involved. They said due to the severity of my attempt, they wouldn't let me go home. Instead, they would be sending me to a mental institution. I cried, begged and pleaded trying to convince them and myself I was fine. A mental hospital? I didn't belong in a place like that. I was desperate. Please don't send me there! I promised to never try anything like that again. I begged, pleaded and did my best to reason with the staff. When I finally realized there wasn't anything I could say to get myself out of the situation, I was in shock. I kept thinking this can't be happening. But it was. So, as I accepted that reality a wave of calm resolution came over me. I looked my parents in the eye and told them I would never speak to them again.

Most of my time there was a blur. I remember lots of crying from myself and the other girls. We had classes because they didn't want us to fall behind in school. As an empath I actually feel the emotions of other people, often without looking at them. I get an incredibly strong sensation of sadness, anger, happiness or anxiety, but I can tell it is coming from someone else. So, one day in class I felt an overwhelming sense of anxiety. I was tense, uncomfortable and my face was hot. I looked around to see where this energy was coming from. As I glanced to my right, I saw a girl who looked a little younger than me, probably about 14. She was a pretty African American girl. Short and slim, with her hair braided into cornrows. She was looking down and focused on her left arm. I leaned forward to see what she was doing only to realize she was picking and scraping her skin. I couldn't make out what she was using, but I saw bright red traces of blood. I swallowed hard as I shuddered and looked away. A few minutes later, I peeked over again hoping she had stopped. Instead she was in a trance, still picking at her skin. This time there was more blood. I chewed on my lip and looked around to see if I was the only one who noticed. Despite my aversion to telling on a fellow patient, I yelled out, "Please stop her, she's not supposed to be doing that!" I just couldn't bear to watch her hurt herself. The nurse came over and grabbed whatever she was using out of her hand. I looked away again, anxious to get out of there. Nights weren't much better. I could always hear her. She screamed and screamed for hours. Banging the walls until the wee hours of the morning, then crying herself to sleep. I wondered what happened to her but was too afraid to ask.

There was another young lady who stood out. I would only see her during our free time. Girls either wandered around aimlessly or sat and conversed with one another. She was a beautiful girl. Shapely with long brown hair and pretty green eyes. She had this beautiful face with the most perfect features. Often, she would sit staring into space. Lost in a world only she had access to. For some reason I was drawn to her. And every now and then, she would be lucid enough to hold a short conversation. Although it was rare for her to speak, whenever she did, I was mesmerized. I wanted to figure her out. What happened? What were her reasons? How did she get there? During a rare clear moment, she began to share her story. One evening she couldn't stop crying.

For weeks prior she had trouble sleeping, often waking up 3 or 4 times a night. She was losing weight from not eating. No matter how hard she tried, her appetite was gone. Her friends and family asked what was wrong, but she wasn't in a space to share. She had given up on things changing, a feeling I understood well. She was drinking daily but this night had downed a half a bottle of Tequila. She grabbed her car keys and stumbled out the door. She kept picking up speed as she drove down a windy road. At some point she knew she was going for it. She floored the gas, screaming before everything went black. She obviously lived, but with consequences I am not sure she ever recovered from. To get that story took several days. Conversations would often drift off, with her disappearing somewhere far too deep for me to reach. Some of the details came from other girls there, probably some was speculation. Filling me in on pieces she couldn't find the words to share or couldn't fully remember. She demonstrated how a suicide attempt can leave you much worse off than dead. There was a deep sadness I felt when I looked at her and a profound feeling she would never be the same. Someone so young and beautiful, just starting her life. Glimpses of a vibrant personality would peek out every so often, before retreating back to whatever world she was living in. A soul trapped inside a fractured mind.

There were so many ladies and everyone had a story. Most people were on meds to either control some emotional issue or to combat whatever they had done to themselves physically. I wanted to scream, "I don't belong here! I'm not like any of you!" The reality is I saw parts of myself in so many of them. It's just easier to point out the flaws in others and ignore our own. I was delusional but had no idea how much I was lying to myself. Luckily, I've always been well-spoken. So, in my first meeting with the psychiatrist, I made up a sob story about a boyfriend who just left me, therefore resulting in my thinking that life was no longer worth living. I claimed that since my stay, I realized my life was so much more important than any relationship. I was sorry for what I had done and would never try it again. At least one part of that was true. I didn't plan on ever trying again. The women I met made me realize that suicide is not an option. The fear of permanent damage scared me far more than death. The rest of what I told the psychiatrist was total bullshit. Taking those pills had nothing to do with a boy. However, that was easier than talking about the real stuff. It was too much to go into my feelings of abandonment and my lifelong battle with depression. I didn't want to share how hurt I was by the lies kids at school made up about me. I couldn't explain how I was shy, but people mistook that as stuck up. How that made me overly conscious of every word I spoke and every move I made. It didn't seem worth it to explain that my high school sweetheart, my first love had cheated on me repeatedly and broke my heart. All that seemed frivolous in the moment. I definitely wasn't going to tell this stranger the real stuff. Like the shame and guilt I carried from the abortion I had a year earlier. That the father, my second love Kevin, had abandoned me in the process. That we had been together over a year. But because we were underage and he kept getting into legal trouble, he was sent across the country to live with his mother in hopes that it would straighten him out. That I didn't find out I was pregnant until after he left. How could I tell this stranger I desperately wanted my child, but I was terrified to do it alone. In the short time we had to talk, I didn't know how to explain to the psychiatrist that my mother, who I hadn't even been living with for very long, told me I either had to have an abortion or I had to get out. I felt betrayed and abandoned by her yet again. Pouring salt onto the wounds I had been carrying from her for so long. How could I share with a stranger I spent a few months staying with friends, desperately hoping I would find a way to keep my baby. I didn't want to relive the shame I felt when I finally gave in and realized if I couldn't take care of myself, how would I take care of a child? So, I went to the abortion clinic, but because I was so far along, I was told it would be a two-day procedure. And when I had the standard ultrasound before the operation, the woman said, "Oh! That's a big healthy baby!" A baby that in my spirit I knew was a boy. That information intensified the mental battle I was having with myself as I went in the operating room on day one. The nurses were chatting over my head, not even acknowledging my presence. Probably indifferent toward another black teenage girl. I suppose they figured it was better to pretend like they were chatting over lunch than acknowledge they were standing over a scared girl about to end the life of her first child. Compassion might have eased the pain of the travesty I was about to commit. Instead, I was surrounded but alone. Inside I was screaming no! I can't do this! I lay on the operating table with sweaty palms and shortness of breath. Tears sliding out of my eyes that I didn't bother to wipe. Not one word of comfort from anyone in the room. I stared at the ceiling as the doctor came in and spread my legs. He slid a cold clamp inside my vagina and placed a grip onto my uterus. As he was getting ready to insert the seaweed stick that would start contractions that evening, I screamed for him to stop. "I can't do this!" I choked out between tears that, until that point, had been ignored. The doctor stepped back, eyes wide as I literally jumped off the table. Hands shaking as I clutched my gown. I felt relieved leaving the room, determined to keep my child no matter what it took. Unfortunately, the relief was short-lived. The solace ended when cramps started the next day. That evening I called the doctor, and they told me that since I had already disturbed my uterus, I would need to come in to complete what I had started. Hearing that was a punch so hard it brought me to my knees. I desperately wanted my child. But the doctor said I had to come back so I did. I felt defeated. My dad brought me back to complete the procedure. I came in the office head down, wanting to get it over with. When I woke up from the surgery, I was completely out of it. The nurses kept shaking me awake. With help, I made it to the waiting room and into the arms of my dad. I was so unsteady that I could barely walk. My dad had to literally pick me up. He carried me downstairs and out of the building. I was in and out of consciousness. The anesthesia wasn't completely worn off. We exited the building as an Indian couple was entering. I could see a look of total shock and terror across both of their faces. The man wrapped his arm around the woman and clutched her tightly. The car was parked directly in front of the building. As my dad placed me gently into the front seat, I flopped my head back onto the head rest. My head rolled to the right and my eyes drifted back at the front door. The couple had paused. They were leaning in closely and talking. My attention moved from them as nausea overtook me. I threw up outside the car door. Once I purged all that would come up, I leaned back against the seat exhausted. I closed my eyes in defeat. I was disgusted with my mom for trying to force me into getting this abortion. I was even more disgusted with myself because I knew that it was my choice, and no matter how hard I tried to resist, in the end, it was I who went through with it. Nobody else. I didn't see if the couple ever went back inside. I thought about them often. Wondering. Praying that my experience was divine intervention for them. Hoping that they made a different choice than I did.

All that led to my stay in the mental hospital. Should I tell this doctor that after my abortion I sunk into the deepest depression I had ever experienced? How would I explain that I cried every time a commercial came on about a baby? That it was hard for me to look into the mirror. I was mad at the unfulfilled promises of help, loved ones made to me, contingent upon going through with the abortion. Ashamed at myself for listening to a mom who, in my eyes, had chosen not to be one. Embarrassed that I had returned shamefully to her house after the whole ordeal. Then one day, I gave up. I decided I would go be with God, my child and my grandpa, who I missed dearly. How could I even begin to share this with the psychiatrist? No, that was way too much to go into. Far too much to uncover. Instead, it was easier to just say I tried to end my life because of a boyfriend. Keep the conversation short. Let it remain simple. The doctor believed me, and I was released the next day. One part of what I said to him was true. That I would never try again. I didn't. I realized after that incident I would always choose life. God had spared my life for a reason. I felt a sense of forgiveness for what I had done and promised to never try again.

Although I didn't spill all my secrets to the psychiatrist, I did realize in that moment I really wanted to live. I realized I was broken. Broken by the shattered relationship with both of my parents. Destroyed by my own actions and countless bad decisions I had yet to forgive myself for. Tormented by my own insecurities. Desperately trying to convince myself that I was worthy of love when I didn't feel that way at all. I understood that my small attempt was an escape, searching for relief. I never wanted to die. I just couldn't imagine continuing life in the pain I was in. Decision must be followed by action. Since I chose life, I had to make a change. I wanted to develop a deep happiness. I didn't yet understand that true happiness must be totally independent of outside people, circumstances and situations. I had to learn a lot and I needed to grow up. I had to build myself up. But first, I had to forgive myself. And I had to forgive the people around me. No one is perfect, not me and not them. I was grateful and wanted to train myself to stay that way. I was grateful I was still alive. Grateful for a new outlook on life. Grateful for my connection to God. He was showing me I could recover from a pain I thought would last forever. I was learning I could grow stronger and part of that was taking responsibility. I was not a victim; I had created a lot of my circumstances. The ones I didn't create were even more special, they were gifts directly from God to make me stronger. Even at my lowest points, I still had my faith. I felt an extra special connection to God and felt his presence often. He had shown me things through my intuition my whole life. Things that shocked the people around me on numerous occasions. He had taken me through a lot, but I was learning to be grateful. I realized if he had taken me that far and I was only 17, God and I had a long way to go. At that moment, I felt empowered. At that moment, I felt ready.

The seeds were planted but change doesn't happen overnight. Despite the hopeful feelings, there were some more rough patches to get through. Ones that were approaching rapidly. I knew what I wanted but was unsure how to achieve it. In order not to get back that low emotionally, I numbed myself even more. I was still running away. I did not have the tools yet to fully heal, transform and grow. Instead, I was getting ready to throw myself into a period of drugs, partying and heartbreak. I had a whole lot of pain coming before I would find my purpose.

I consider that our present sufferings aren't worthy to be compared to the glory that is within us.

Romans 8:18

Chapter 3- Wild

The next chapter of my life started with good intentions but no direction. I was young, angry and wild. It was a recipe for disaster and a set up for trauma. I was getting ready to make some of the biggest mistakes of my life, which would also be some of the most valuable lessons I would ever learn. After the abortion and subsequent suicide attempt, I went back to my mom's house briefly. Disappointment wasn't new and I thought I could stay there until I turned 18. At this point, I passed the CHSPE, which is the California equivalent of a GED. I only had about a year left to tough it out at my mom's. I was excited about starting early at a local community college. I wanted to get on with my life and away from the trauma I was trying to forget. My secret weapon was my stepdad Kenny who was the coolest man you'll ever meet. He had been with my mom for so long that I always knew him to be in my life. He taught me how to drive, listened to my boy problems and looked the other way when I would sneak out. My mom worked a lot. When she was home, she was usually in her room. So, I had friends and cousins that would come over all the time. We would cook, I would do their hair and we would stay up all night laughing and talking. In my mother's defense she did try to implement some rules, but it was too late. My feelings were that 16 was too late to start raising me. I wanted to be a roommate with all the adult freedom and none of the responsibilities. Obviously, that wasn't going to work, especially since I was paying zero percent of the bills, a fact I conveniently ignored. There was tension and everything was coming to a boiling point. Shortly after I came home, we got into a huge fight. I lost control and was screaming and cursing at my mom. Kenny, my big friendly giant (who was also an ex-boxer) had to kick down my door and restrain me while my mother called the police. She wanted them to come to take me to juvenile hall. Since I hadn't really committed a crime; my understanding was that she would pay them to hold me. I still don't know if that is true or if it is just what she said to scare me. Either way, I wasn't keen on being put back in a facility. My stint at the mental institution was still fresh. I was hurt, angry and wasn't allowing anyone to tell me what to do. I was too close to grown and had my own plans. I was still enjoying weed and ecstasy regularly and loved the way they both felt. I was taking it more and more. I didn't see I had lost control. Ecstasy heightened my emotions and kept me up for hours. That's not a good combination when you're trying to stay calm. So, when I heard juvenile hall, I climbed out of my second-story bedroom window and ran away. I saw a police car go by several times, I assumed looking for me. I was literally in the bushes. Hiding in the dirt and leaves, heart pounding because I was high with no plans and nowhere to go. All I had was a determination to never go back to my mom's. Again, in this period, I was blind to my own faults. I felt betrayed by my mom again. Yet I was blind to the most obvious thing, which was that I had betrayed myself with my actions and choices. I had yet to take any real responsibility for the part I played in how my life was going. At the end of the day, we are responsible for how our lives go. We always have a choice in every situation and I should have chosen better. I got pregnant. I went through with the abortion. I was responsible. Of course, none of that crossed my mind as I waited for the flashing lights to disappear. It didn't take long for the police to give up, and I walked to the bus stop without a real plan.

Difficult situations are a part of life. I needed to understand that I always had a choice. I could have worked through the pain instead of being a victim to it. I could have been the love I felt I was missing. Instead, I chose to be angry. I ignored the fact that I had made a lot of bad choices for myself and was suffering the consequences. I was so stuck in the why me victim mentality, that I was torturing myself. I caused myself so much suffering because I hadn't learned how to move through the pain. Yes, trauma hurts. The consequential pain is real and should be expressed, seen and honored. But avoiding healing only prolongs suffering. I had not chosen to learn the lessons and use them as a catalyst to grow and be better. I had not developed the mindset and perspective needed to rise above the mess.

That night I went to a friend's house and stayed for about a week. I knew that couldn't be a long-term solution. If I was choosing to be on my own for an extended period, I would need to be responsible for the basics. I simply wasn't comfortable asking someone else for long-term help with food and shelter, even if they were a friend. With every fiber of my being I wanted to prove everyone wrong. I felt like it was me against the world, but I had God on my side and with him I could not fail. I believe I went about 6 months without speaking to my parents. However, Kenny had always been a confidant so I kept in touch with him. I can not overstate the value, love, understanding and kindness Kenny has always added to my life. He taught me how to drive. At 14 we began to sneak out for lessons. He would take me to an empty backstreet where I could practice. Once I started getting good, he let me practice on the street. I was so focused on not hitting cars that it took me a while to remember to look out for pedestrians. Kenny would scream "Girl watch out!" as I slammed on the brakes. Once I was in the turning lane. My light was red but the cars next to me had a green. Looking at the wrong light I took off. Cars screeched and honked as I pulled into the intersection. I was so scared I slammed on the brakes, stopping in the middle of the street. "Go! Go! Go! Are you trying to kill us?" Kenny laughed but I noticed the beads of sweat forming. Despite it all he remained patient. He was always down to listen to me vent, giving me honest advice and a man's perspective. He was a phone call away, picking me up countless times from hanging out somewhere I wasn't supposed to be. He was always there for me. My friends used to joke and call him a real-life superhero. We were partying every weekend and Kenny was there to rescue us every weekend as well. As silly young girls, we would go to parties knowing we did not have a way back. Public transportation would not be running by the time we got out and he would literally come to whatever city we ended up in, pile 7 girls into a 4-door Volvo and take us all home. He rescued us from places like Sacramento, Berkeley and San Jose. Once we were in San Francisco. It was 5 of us and the party got shot up. We called him and he was still at work. We told him we would walk towards home, until he got off. Over an hour later we saw headlights in the distance, praying it was him. We ran to his car, grateful for the safety and warmth. Of course, there were times he wasn't available. That led to some interesting situations. One evening I was out with a friend at a party. Around 11 I turned to Amber reminding her we needed to find a ride. We started looking for anyone we recognized. I found one girl I knew from school, but she was going in a different direction. Amber ran into a friend of hers, but the car was full. By the time the party ended we still didn't have a way home. Thank God for tennis shoes. We were walking for about 15 minutes, unsure of how we were going to get back, when a car pulled up next to us. The driver called out "Hey love, you ok?". I locked eyes with Amber before responding "No. We are stuck and need to get home to Richmond." He offered us a ride. Grateful we ran up to the car. Amber leaned over and whispered "Ohhh the passenger is cuttteeee." before climbing in the seat behind the driver. For the first few minutes we all bobbed our heads to the music. The driver looked in his rear view mirror. Catching his eye she smiled and said "Hi, I'm Amber". "Nice to meet you. My name's Jamal". He returned her smile and began making conversation. The passenger started to chat with me. She leaned over and mumbled "Ugh, you always get the cute ones." I responded with a laugh. He looked a little short but he was cute. Plus you can't get a good gauge of height when someone is sitting down. What I could see was that he was chocolate with a nice fade and handsome features. We were laughing and vibing, having a good conversation. The ride went smoothly but when we arrived in Richmond the car pulled up to a random building.

"Why are we here? My house is off South 23rd." I asked.

"Oh I need to grab something from my house." Jamal responded.

"It's ok we can wait in the car."

"Nah I don't know yall, you have to come inside and then we will take you home. I'm not cool with leaving yall in my car"

Aaron turned to me "It's good. Don't worry. We just have to grab something and then we will take you home."

I looked at Amber, knowing what they were trying to pull. I recognized the area and realized we could walk from there. Amber and Jamal were on the same side of the car. When they got out he draped his arm over her shoulders. I reluctantly climbed out of my side, shivering as I stepped back into the cold. As I turned towards Amber, Aaron called out. "Wait up Tash." I turned my head, prepared to say bye and maybe exchange numbers, but didn't see him. My forehead wrinkled as I looked around. Where did he go? Aaron stepped around the car and I felt an arm slide around my waist. His head rested directly on my side. I looked down and my eyes widened. Thank God we weren't face to face as I tried to keep my composure. How did I not realize he was a little person? No judgement on my end but it caught me off guard. I glanced in Amber's direction and saw her face was flushed. I bit my lip and did my best to avoid making eye contact. I knew if we looked at each other we would both lose it. Determined to keep a straight face I started fiddling with my shirt.

"Come on baby lets go inside."

"Uhhhhh no that's ok." I quickly responded for both of us.

"Why not?"

"I'm good. We can walk from here."

I grabbed Amber's arm pulling her down the street. Once we were about a block away she turned to me "Well I didn't see that coming."

"Girl I couldn't even tell."

We laughed hysterically the whole way home. Incidents like that made us appreciate Kenny even more. I'm sure he got tired of rescuing us, but it never showed. There's a family saying that if you can't get along with Kenny, you can't get along with anyone. I thank God for his presence in my life, especially during that time.

In the midst of the madness, I enrolled in the local community college and signed up for fee waivers and grants. I used that money for food and to keep me afloat. Because I was too young to rent an apartment, and did not have much money, I slept on buses. I would wait for the 72, the bus with the longest route, and ride it all night.

It crossed the span of about four cities from Oakland to Richmond. There was a bus driver who was a kind middle-aged black man. He let me stay on the bus even during his breaks. He never asked any questions. But he noticed I rode his bus back and forth all night. So eventually he let me stay in the back and sleep while he took his breaks. It was a warm, safe refuge. At about 5 am I would get off the bus and go into a local coffee shop that opened super early. The owners were friendly and allowed me to eat and then lay my head on the table and sleep for about an hour. From there, I would make my way to school. Some days I snuck into my dad's house while he was at work to shower and nap. The truth is he would have never turned me away, but my pride wouldn't allow me to ask. It was hard, but I was making it work. I was clean, had nice clothes and never ever asked strangers for money or loitered. So, from the outside looking in, no one would know that I was homeless (except the bus driver and the owner of the local coffee shop). For food, I was creative. I read a book called Fast Food Nation in high school that turned me off from fast food. So even at my lowest, I refused to eat from places like McDonalds and Wendy's. I patronized small mom and pop joints. I would eat any form of potatoes because of how well they would fill you up. Bread and sandwiches were also cheap fillers. Tacos were another favorite, and there are tons of taco trucks throughout Oakland, so it was convenient. I was finding ways to make do with what I had. I learned resourcefulness, a new level of appreciation and how to survive.

During that time, I got into a terrible pattern of signing up for tons of classes, doing well in the beginning, and then getting too high too often and dropping out before the end of the semester. I did complete some classes but overall found it hard to focus. Eventually I took a break from school. I began to work a variety of jobs from Blockbuster to the local gas station, providing enough money to get by. It was also during this time I met someone special who changed the way I looked at life and love. She was tall with a medium build, tan skin and hazel eyes. Her hair was long with these beautiful curls. She was mixed with black and Mexican, and she was gorgeous. Every time I saw her, I got butterflies. When she asked me for my number I just melted. Within a few months, I was in deep like. We could talk for hours about anything. We would laugh, joke and have fun. It was different than with my friends. I was attracted to her, and it was obvious she was attracted to me too. Before then, I had never even come close to a same-sex relationship. Jessica changed that. After the first time we had sex, I was in love. It was such a different experience. The softness of her body, the way my hands would caress her curves. Large, supple breasts I couldn't stay away from. It was not only my first time having intimate feelings for a woman, but it was also my first time having sex with one. Oral sex became something I enjoyed for the first time. She took her time with my body. She slowly kissed, rubbed, teased and touched every area. We explored everything from a strap on to scissoring. The sex was electrifying and I was hooked. She was my first girlfriend but definitely wouldn't be my last. I was comfortable with her in private, but in public was another story. Even in the grocery store, I felt like everyone was looking at us. I remember being so scared to tell anyone for fear of being judged. When I came out to my dad, his exact words were, "I don't give a shit who you are with as long as they treat you right." That level of love and acceptance sums up my dad perfectly. It also gave me the confidence to follow my heart and be me. I began to be ok with showing affection in public. I didn't care what anyone thought. That also brought Jessica and I closer. She had been out for years and was not accustomed to hiding who she was. She taught me a new level of self acceptance. Things were looking up with us. But between Jessica, different jobs and being homeless, school was not a consistent priority. My life was an odd mix. I was high every day, losing weight and falling off track. I knew that I needed to be clean to have the life I wanted to live, but it is so much easier said than done. Drugs are a distraction. Even love can be a distraction. Addictions in general, are a desperate attempt to ignore or forget the things too painful to face. By trying to self medicate and band-aid my wounds, I was floundering around without getting anything done. Focusing on Jessica, gave me an out from focusing on myself.

Eventually Jessica and I drifted apart and I reconnected with Eric. We grew up in the church together. Our families were friends and I had a crush on him when we were younger. But before we could even go on a date or see each other in person we got into a stupid argument. He told a mutual friend I bought him a pair of shoes, which I did not. I called him on three-way, confronted him and he denied it. He was embarrassed to be called out on a lie. I didn't want to entertain someone that was making things up about me, regardless of how small they may have been. It was so ridiculous I decided not to pursue a relationship with him and quickly shoved him out my mind. A week later I was at a party with a friend when Eric called my phone "B**ch f*ck you! I'm going to have my sister beat yo ass!" I had no idea what he was so upset about. Our argument was not serious. But I was young, immature and in my ego. So, I responded "F*ck you and that b**ch. I don't like her anyway." I then told him where I was and waited for them to arrive. In hindsight I am amazed at my own ignorance. Why would I think that was a smart way to handle the situation? About 20 minutes later my phone rang again.

"I hope you're ready to die."

"Huh? What are you talking about?"

"I'm bout to shoot you"

My mouth dropped open. My chest constricted and my eyes darted around.

"Please let my friend go. She doesn't have anything to do with this." I was praying this was a joke despite the seriousness in his voice. But if it wasn't, I couldn't let my friend suffer the consequences. I turned to Helen and my voice cracked "He has a gun. I'm not fighting his sister. He tricked me into telling him where I was. You have to leave and I have to get out of here."

"No Tash."

I got loud. "This is serious! You have to go right now!"

"I love you Tash I'm not leaving you."

It was like time slowed down. I didn't see Eric but I knew we needed to get away. We walked up to Telegraph which is a busy street. We kept anxiously looking over our shoulders as we tried to keep up our pace. My legs were cramping and I was beginning to lose my breath. "Come on Helen we have to keep moving". I looked to my right and stopped in my tracks. There was a car full of men, Eric was in the back seat. He had on a black hoodie and a beanie. His eyes were blank, as if his soul had left his body. He had a slight grin, like he was having fun. The window was down and a gun was pointed at us. I grabbed Helens hand and yanked her down to the ground, using a car to shield our bodies. My heart was pounding as I looked up and down the block. I thought God please help us and tried to formulate a plan. "Ok." I whispered "We are going to run to the corner and go left. We have to hop the fence to the first house we see and find somewhere to hide. If we can't, we'll run through their backyard until we find somewhere to go. We too out in the open". Helen gripped my hand tighter and nodded. I took a deep breath and we took off running. The car skirted off after us as we hit a left at the corner. There were big buildings (and no fence) on our left. It just so happened to be a huge semi truck parked on the right, which we used as a shield. The car slammed on the brakes near the front of the truck, then threw the car in reverse back to the corner. We stayed put, praying he wouldn't get out of the car. They then drove forward, tires screeching down the street. I knew they were going to come back around the block so we turned and sprinted as fast as we could, into a liquor store. We ran to the back, hiding in the furthest corner we could find. Beads of sweat were running down my face as I tried to figure out what to do. I was so used to dealing with racism from the police, that calling them didn't cross my mind. Instead, I called Rene and Shep, who I knew lived about 15 blocks away. We frantically told them the story and begged them to come help us. We did not move from that spot until they arrived. They ran into the store sweating, t-shirts damp and out of breath. They had no guns, weapons or car. But I felt better with their presence. We were reluctant to leave the store but the owners were growing impatient. They didn't call the police either. I was on the verge of tears as we exited together. We walked a half a block to the nearest bus stop, looking around frantically for any sign of the car. Granted, he never fired the weapon, but seeing the gun pointed at me still had me shaking. I wanted to call him and ask why, beg him to stop, but there was no use. He enjoyed our fear. Within 10 minutes the car pulled up on us. I grabbed Rene terrified and ready to run. The car was paused in the middle of the street, right on the corner of 27th and Telegraph. All 5 men were staring directly at us. I felt open, vulnerable and desperate to get away. "Should we run behind Taco Bell?" I whispered. Helen clutched my arm as Shep ran up to the car. "N***a is it a problem?". Before he could reach the vehicle they pulled off. I was shaking until I got home.

Rene and Shep saved our lives. A few years later Eric got into an argument with the mother of his child. He texted her, telling her he was going to kill her and her boyfriend. He lay in the bushes outside of her apartment and waited. When they exited her home, he shot and killed them both. I learned so many hard lessons through Eric. You don't know what people are capable of. Avoid confrontations at all costs. I never imagined he would pull a gun on me. We never had sex, we never even kissed. The argument was beyond petty. Still, I should not have told him where I was. My ego could have cost me my life. Even worse, it could have cost my friend hers. I will never forget Helen staying by my side and I thank God for sparing our lives.

The following year I turned 18 and two things happened that changed my life dramatically. The first was receiving $5'000 from a trust fund left to me by my grandpa Raymond. I used that money to purchase a car, which was an absolute Godsend. My car became my home. The trunk became my closet and the back seat became my bed. I hung out with friends and took long drives to clear my mind. I took tons of road trips to LA and Vegas whenever I had a few days off of work. I was taking a break from school and having lots of fun. My car was my safety and security. It kept me from sleeping on the bus or walking around for endless hours at night. I was so relieved to no longer face the dangers that came in the evenings. Like the one time I was walking to the bus stop that was my nightly route. A Caucasian man in a white 4 door sedan began to follow me. He screamed out things that terrified me. "Wait till I catch you! Watch what I'm going to do to you." He followed me for about 20 minutes. I did not know this man and had no weapons to protect me. The sharpest thing in my backpack was a book. The anger and disgust he was spewing towards me had me in fear for my life. There was no one around to help me. Eventually, I saw a police officer and ran over to him crying hysterically. I asked him to drop me off down the street at my friend's house. I kept that as a last resort for the evenings I couldn't stand to be out. Incidents like this taught me just how dangerous it was to be homeless as a young woman. Sleeping outside alone wasn't an option. I could be raped or killed. Which is why I was so grateful to have good friends like James and his amazing family. Anytime I couldn't take it, they let me stay over. At one point I even moved in for about 6 months. James and I took over the living room and I did hair in exchange. Despite my gratitude, I didn't want to be a burden on anyone, and I loved the freedom my car gave me.

My car was also a gateway to what became one of my favorite pastimes. Side shows. If you lived in Oakland anytime from the 80's to the 2000s, side shows were probably a part of your life. It was like a big street party. Cars would get in a long line, blast their music and race up and down the street. Scrapers on rims, with speakers blasting E-40, Too Short, The Team, Keak the Sneak and Keyshia Cole. After about 20 minutes of driving back to back down long streets, we would randomly stop at a gas station. Everyone would hop out of the car and go dumb (the 2004 Oakland term for dance and shake your dreads), talk, smoke and hangout. The streets would be packed with cars and people. That it is until a fight broke out or someone started shooting. It was expected so we strategically parked in a position where we could get out. We were never backed in a corner behind other cars. We were also never fully out in the open. Several times we ended up crouching behind cars to avoid the people shooting back and forth. One evening the gun fire started. Everyone scattered as we turned to run back to our car. Hundreds of people reduced to a handful in a matter of seconds. I looked out to the intersection and saw a man drop. He was tall, with caramel skin and a fade. His body hit the pavement but in a matter of seconds he popped back up. He was running, but now with a limp. He must have been shot in his leg. Pop! Pop! Pop! He dropped back to the ground, he was hit again. This time I couldn't see where he was hurt. I couldn't believe it. Was this man about to get murdered in front of me? Refusing to give up, he leapt up and kept running. He was moving slower this time. Cars were screeching off in every direction. His friends were gone. He was banging on the windows of every passing car, begging them to let him in. Car after car ignored him. Finally, a car full of women stopped. The back door opened and he dove into the back seat. They peeled off so fast the tires were screeching. I can still see the look on his face.

One evening I was the passenger at a sideshow. One of my good friends Natalie was driving. It was her and her boyfriend in the front. I sat in the middle seat in the back. Even for us, she was driving wild. Twice she was a few inches from hitting a car. We were coming down MacArthur, approaching 98th. Both are busy streets. I was in the back rolling a blunt. Running red lights was common during sideshows, everyone did it. But when you are at the cross of two major intersections, traffic would stop. There were too many cars in every direction. I looked up ahead and saw a red light. Cars were backed up about a block. Instead of slowing down she sped up and hopped on the opposite side of the street, thinking she could swerve back over before the light turned green. There wasn't enough time. Now traffic was moving and 2 rows of cars were driving head on in our direction. I knew we were going to crash but didn't have time to get my seat belt on. She swerved to the left, hopping the sidewalk. We drove through a fence and everything went black. "Get her!" I heard someone scream. I came fully to as I was being pulled out of the car. I had flown from the backseat into her air bag. Thank God for those because I would have gone right through the window. As I sat on the front lawn, waiting for Kenny to pick us up, I looked at the car. We had crashed into the side of a house and I was grateful not to even have a cut. That didn't stop us from going to sideshows. In retrospect, I don't know how we normalized the amount of craziness, violence and gunfire. At the time it was just a part of life. At their most popular times, there would be hundreds of cars, stopped for hours in the middle of the street. We would lock our cars and get out, dancing in the street and having fun. Police and even helicopters would be there, but they were nothing more than a witness and a visual deterrent to violence. My favorite part was racing my Cutlass up and down the street. Music blasting, with my friends literally hanging out the window. During those days, I was taking ecstasy every single night. Riding out with my best friend Tasha (yes, we have the same name), having the time of our lives. That high allowed me to party for hours without getting tired. I was still homeless with nowhere to go, so rushing home was never an issue. At the end of the night, which often ended around 3 or 4 in the morning, I would drive to a nice neighborhood and crawl in the back of my car and go to sleep. I kept a dark blanket in the car to help me blend into the seats. And I always slept in the driver's seat in case I needed to react quickly. Several times I got woken up by a police officer tapping on my window. It is really difficult to be homeless. You don't want to sleep on the streets because of the obvious dangers. In a vehicle there's nowhere to park and sleep without being bothered. The hood is dangerous to park your car without being completely on guard. Once I was parked in West Oakland just trying to get a few hours of sleep. A friend was with me. I was jolted awake by him shaking me and yelling "Wake up, we have to go!" I was tired, out of it and confused. He told me a car passed by us slowly several times. There were two men who were looking in the car. The way they had positioned themselves, it seemed like they might be attempting to rob us. I turned the car on as quickly as I could. We were squeezed into a tight space. In my desperation to get out I hit the cars in front and behind me before pulling off as fast as I could. That was the risk of those neighborhoods. On the other hand, when you park in nice areas, the residents call the police on you. There's nowhere you belong. You are trying to exist undetected and without bothering anyone. It's an extraordinarily uncomfortable way to live.

To ignore the current circumstances, I liked to stay high, busy and have fun as much as possible. I figured I might as well make the most out of the situation. If we weren't driving turnt up in a sideshow, we were going to what they called Black Saturdays. They were essentially a hood party for the 15-20-year-old crowd. There was a party promoter who hosted these parties all over the bay area. They would rent out anything from a warehouse to a church and turn it out. They had great music and we danced all night, but they also got shot up almost every single time. You wore tennis shoes because you expected to run out of there. Again, it boggles my mind what I normalized. Drugs didn't help. Between ecstasy and weed, I wasn't thinking straight. One evening we were at a black Saturday which was being held in a warehouse in Berkeley. The night was going as usual. A dark room with loud music and the consistent smell of weed. Lots of young, hot, sweaty bodies pressed together. All of a sudden, we heard a gunshot and the crowd scattered in opposite directions. I lost sight of my friends as I took off running. I heard a Pop! Pop! Pop! In front of me. I froze, then another Pop! Behind me. A couple of shots was a normal way to signal the end of the night at a Black Saturday, but back and forth gunfire was not. I was terrified. I had no idea which way to go. It was dark and I could barely see. I scanned the area around me and saw a group of people hiding in a small closet-like area off to the side. The look on their faces was pure terror. I jumped in with them, squeezing my body between theirs. I gripped the arm of a stranger, praying we all made it out alive. I don't remember how long we hid there, but we stayed until we heard "Berkeley police!! Come out with your hands in the air." We were all relieved and walked out slowly, hands raised. The cool air felt so good and I don't know if I had ever been so happy to see the police in my life. That was the last Black Saturday I ever went to. I had been to so many that ended in gunshots, but something about that night ended my desire to ever go to another one again. I was very aware God kept saving my life, and I didn't want to keep making him work so hard.

I'd like to say I calmed down completely after that, but it isn't true. I did slow down and was more cautious of the situations I put myself in. However, that was around the time the second life-changing situation happened. I was working at a local target. It was before the store opened, so we were just putting shelving units together. This was before the products were even brought into the store. My supervisor was a young black lady around my age. From our first interaction, it was clear we weren't a good match. I felt like she was rude, condescending and aggressive. The way she spoke to the employees under her was uncalled for. She would make up complete lies to our managers, not just about me but about several other employees as well. A few of these people were fired. In the break room, I would overhear her calling me a bitch, not even trying to be discreet. Now remember, at this time I was still homeless. Most people my age were working for spending money. They clicked up like it was a high school class versus a job where you were getting paid. I was working to survive. I had done hair in high school and still did a few clients on the side. But this job was my main source of income. It was how I had money for food. Because of that I tried to ignore her. In retrospect I should have tried to speak to her, maybe we could have even been friends. Instead, the tension grew. One day before work I walked in the break room. I noticed her but did not speak. I was putting my backpack in my locker, preparing for my shift. As I stuffed it inside, I realized I didn't have my cell phone. I ran back outside, hoping the cab that dropped me off had not left. Not only were they gone, but when I returned my backpack was missing. So was she. In my rush, I forgot to close the locker. She was the only one in there and had been harassing me already for months. So, it wasn't difficult to figure out she took it. The issue was that my backpack had my diary, clothes and personal belongings. Even my social security card was in there. I was angry that I had so little to my name, and it had been stolen. I was furious that my most personal thoughts and struggles could be accessed. I felt violated. But I needed the job too badly to make a scene. I promised myself that if she ever got me fired, I would come back up there and confront her about all that she had done. Within a week, it happened. She made up lies to my higher-up managers, who got me fired. I was furious. I walked around the store looking for her, but they said she left early. I stayed the night at my friend James' house. I smoked and tried to talk it out and calm down. I woke up the next morning just as angry. I just could not let it go. I was young and immature. Despite the situation, I could have focused on the fact that everything happens for a reason. I could have kept my mind on moving towards better opportunities. Instead, I begged James to come with me to the job and I called another friend Jared to give us a ride. We waited for her to arrive, and I told them not to get out of the car. When she pulled up, I got out of the car alone and confronted her. Within a few minutes, we were outside fighting. I made the mistake of smoking before I went. Weed slows you down. So, in the beginning, I was having a little trouble. She was definitely getting in more hits than I was. I laugh looking back at it because she caught me with a hit so hard, I said she knocked the high out of me. At that moment, I decided there was no way she was going to steal from me, lie about me, get me fired and beat me up. It was just too much. After that extra hard hit, I blacked out and took control of the fight. By the time I came to, she was crouching down and I was hitting her in her head. At that point, I was even madder she wouldn't keep fighting back. I thought I was disgusted with her but in reality I was disgusted with myself. The fight was over. I jogged back to the car, and we took off. Violence never ever helps a situation. I should have been mature enough to walk away from her and that job without looking back. Instead, I was focused on the sum of what was taken from me. I was thinking about how after work, I would go and spend $1.75 on a bag of French fries from a local burger joint, and that would be my dinner. I was thinking about the hurt, pain and difficulty of my lifestyle. None of that was her fault. But that was compounded with the upset of losing my job based on lies. At that moment, I felt like a physical fight was the only way to go. I did not know that she went inside and lied to the managers, saying me and several other girls beat her up. A few weeks later, I got pulled over for running a stop sign. The police officer asked me to step outside to sign the ticket. I thought that was odd. As soon as I exited the car he put me in handcuffs. I went to jail on a warrant for assault and battery. Luckily, I got a great public defender who found the working security tapes outside of the Target, proving the fight was one on one. She also got a copy of my complaint against her. Once this was presented in court my charges were reduced. I spent 21 days in jail and was released.

You would think that would have been the wake-up call I needed. Instead, I went to jail 2 more times over the next few years. It really is sad looking back, but I wasn't that bothered. I had nothing going for myself. I was still homeless, sleeping in my car. I was sad, mad and angry at the world. That's what lack of accountability will do to you. It causes you to look at everyone but yourself. It causes you to feel justified in making excuses instead of making it happen. It's frustrating when you want to change your life but aren't sure how. My anger grew at night. It was so very cold. Even in the car, under blankets, the freezing temperatures would wake me up every morning around 2 am. I was getting high around the clock to make life bearable, without realizing that getting high was just making life harder. I worked a variety of retail jobs. Working hours and hours for a small check and even smaller respect. What I learned was that I wouldn't last long in these settings and desired a career with respect and good pay. Minutes felt like hours in retail, and I'd rather eat chalk than spend a lifetime running a register. My mind was always moving and sitting still wasn't my strong suit. What I did still enjoy was doing hair. It was a welcome relief. I would go to the client's home, have a good time doing their hair, and if I was really lucky, they would offer me something to eat. I had a lot of Eritrean clients. They were my favorites because they love to feed you. They made injera and meat dishes from scratch. It was spicy but delicious. I became used to the strong smell of coffee, which they would make from fresh coffee beans. They were being hospitable and had no idea that it was often my only meal of the day. I would be in no rush to leave the warm comfort of my client's homes, many of whom became like family. At that time, I was starting to have more and more people calling to get their hair done. So, after work and off days were often spent driving from client to client, quite often with Tasha there to assist me. I did not see it at the time, but God was preparing me in so many ways for what was to come.

I felt this strong, intense connection to God through all that I went through. Even at my worst, I knew I was in a temporary season that I needed to shake. This would not be the end of my story. I felt it in my spirit that my life would serve a higher purpose. I was stuck and depressed, but I had faith it would change. God reminded me he was always with me. One major way was through my intuition. It was my connection to God, and it felt like a direct line. A secret conversation I was so lucky to be a part of. There are many examples of how my intuition saved my life. Once I was in the car with my boyfriend at the time Rene and my cousin Monica. We were driving in Oakland alongside the freeway. It was late at night and Rene was driving while I was in the back seat asleep. "Stopppppppppp!!!!!!" I heard myself scream as Rene slammed on the brakes. It was almost an out of body experience as I realized the voice was coming from me. "What the fuck is wrong with you, cousin?" Monica asked. I was quiet because, in all honesty, I didn't know. We paused in the middle of the street with everyone slightly confused. A few seconds later, a car came flying from the left, off the side of the freeway. Let's be clear; they did not drive off the exit. It looked as if they lost control, veered to a sharp right and drove down a short hill off the side of the freeway. The car flew right past our front bumper, slamming into a parked car slightly to our right. This vehicle caused a ricochet where 3 parked cars were hit. Had we kept driving, he might have t-boned our car. At the speed he was going, he could have killed any of us on impact. Thankfully no one was in the other cars, but we were scared for the driver. We sat there in shock for a few minutes until the driver door opened, and the driver stumbled out of the car, clearly drunk. He plopped to the ground and lit a cigarette. We laughed, realizing he was fine. The commotion was so loud several people had come out of their homes. They stood on balconies, phones in hand as we drove away. Either God, my angels or my spirit guides saved our lives that day. To wake me out of my sleep screaming is something I never forgot and never took for granted. When I say God is my friend, protector and confidant, I mean it.

I do think it's important to clarify a few things about my perspective. I am a very liberal and open person who has studied multiple religions. In my opinion there is wisdom and truth in each one, yet none have all the answers. As humans, how could we fully grasp all the wonders of the world? So, for me, it doesn't matter if we call that energy God, Allah, the one, etc. What matters is that I acknowledge this amazing spirit, presence and connection. I believe in energy, healing crystals and God. God is what I choose to call the essence I've experienced my whole life because I grew up in the church. Yet it is important to state that in no way am I trying to dismiss what anyone else believes in, connects to or resonates with. I respect all faiths and beliefs.

So, let's get back to it. Another time I kept having a dream about a certain date Rene shouldn't go outside. I told him the date and begged him to stay in for the day. I didn't know what would happen, but I was scared. At this point, he had enough experiences with me to believe what I was sensing. He stayed inside the entire day. Unfortunately, he underestimated how much he was going to smoke. Late that evening, he walked to the 7-eleven to get a swisher and some snacks. He exited the store, walking right behind another young man. They turned and headed in the same direction. The stranger started up a hill with Rene a few feet behind. What neither of them realized was a car was following the man in front of Rene. The occupants of that vehicle must have assumed they were together. Someone in the car shot at them both and Rene took off running. When the car screeched off, he jumped in the back of a pick-up truck to hide. He called me, whispering and panting into the phone. He told me what happened and I drove to him as fast as I could, thanking God the whole way he was ok. We all have intuition. It is a gift God has given to each and every one of us. Some people have dreams. Others have visual premonitions. Some people hear things, others just know. It is there for everyone. But for some it's more powerful than others. Like a muscle, it grows stronger with practice. The more we listen to and honor that spiritual connection, the deeper it becomes.

Not too long after this, Rene and I split up but remained friends. A few months after the split, I was visiting my friend Tasha and she mentioned her brother Ricky was interested in me. I had always been super attracted to him, so we exchanged numbers. We hung out and didn't stop for the next 5 years. I had always connected easily with people. I thrived off deep conversations and deeper connections. Yet even for me, this was different. We just vibed. We could talk for hours about absolutely anything. I was still homeless. I was still addicted to ecstasy. I still battled depression. But he didn't judge me. I had always been slim, but I was an unhealthy skinny. Yet he thought I was beautiful. In many ways I was at my worst, yet he accepted me. He genuinely supported me, and I supported him. We didn't have money, but we had each other. We slept in my car together, and I no longer felt alone. I knew I had someone who had my back 100%. We both battled addiction, but we wanted more out of life. We wanted to break free of the chains that bound us. Chains of addiction and unresolved hurt and pain. Self-imposed chains. We did not realize that only we had the key to free ourselves. Being with Ricky made me want more for myself and more for us as a couple. We talked about our hopes and dreams for the future. We supported and understood each other in a unique way. During that time, I also started getting back closer to my family. As I did the work of healing and forgiving myself, forgiving everyone else became so much easier. Our feelings about other people are often a reflection of our feelings about ourselves. When we are kind to ourselves, we are naturally more kind to others. When we look for our own faults, we are quicker to see the faults in others. When we want more love, goodness and kindness from the outside world, we must first give that to ourselves. We are energetic beings. We will experience what we are.

Early on, Ricky proved his loyalty. I rented a hotel room for my cousin's birthday. There were about 8 people in the room hanging out. We were smoking, drinking and popping E pills. We had the music up and we were having a good time. At some point, someone pulled out a gun to show off. They passed it around the room. It seemed as if everyone except Ricky and I were impressed. Guns make me extremely uncomfortable and I immediately demanded they put it away. Someone tucked it under the mattress. It was just in time because less than 10 minutes later, we got a knock on the door. It was the Berkeley police department. Two female cops showed up, told us we were being too loud, and demanded we leave. Had we not been high with a gun in the room I would have asked why we didn't get a courtesy warning. Instead, we grabbed our belongings and rushed out. Once we vacated the premises, I asked the owner of the gun if he had grabbed it. He said no and my heart dropped. The room was in my name. What if the gun was dirty? Meaning what if it had been used in a crime. I barely knew this guy; he was a friend of a friend and I did not want to be tied to anything he might have done. We knew the cleaning ladies would find it as soon as they went to make the bed. They would immediately turn it over to the police. The only option was to get the gun out of the room. We started with the easiest option, which was to call the hotel and ask if we could retrieve something we left. The answer was no. We sat and tried to figure out what to do. Do we break a window and get in? Do we rush the cleaning ladies in the morning? Everyone seemed scared and said we should just leave the gun. Easy to say when your ID wasn't used to get the room. I wasn't ready to bear the weight of any possible consequences. Everyone went home and Ricky and I were left to figure it out. Early the next morning we came back to the motel. As soon as the cleaning ladies opened the room we ran up. I talked to them while Ricky walked inside and grabbed the gun. I don't think the ladies even knew what he grabbed. He showed me right then and there that he would have my back.

Shortly after that I had an experience I wished he was there for. One evening I was in North Richmond, riding with Natalie and her sister. It was late and dark in a dangerous neighborhood. Natalie had tinted windows on her car. Her sister kept urging her to roll them down but she refused. We were smoking and playing loud music, oblivious to our surroundings. Suddenly we saw headlights driving straight towards us. I screamed and clutched my seatbelt as a black Honda cut us off. A man hopped out the front seat. He ran up to the drivers window with a large black gun aimed at Natalie's head.

"Bitch roll the fucking windows down!"

I stared silently. There was nothing I could do or say.

Natalie's sister screamed out "Ay ay ay! It's me! My sis and her patnas are just taking me home!"

"You lucky blood. Tell this dumb ass bitch not to drive through here with these fucking tinted windows. They hit me immediately when yall crossed the train tracks. It's bad. Know where the fuck you at and act accordingly!"

We dropped her off, hearts still beating out of control. Our windows were down until we left the area. There was a whole operation. North Richmond was known for drugs, guns and one of the highest murder rates in the country. They had an elaborate system of communication and control. They talked through the Nextel phones, which had a walkie talkie feature. When any unknown vehicle came in the area, they knew. They were protecting their own and a car with tinted windows and several occupants was a threat. A lot of people died during those years and we were lucky we weren't one of them. It's been around 15 years since that incident and I haven't been back to North Richmond since.

I always felt better when Ricky was around. One afternoon we walked into a local corner store. He was in the back grabbing a few items while I walked to the front to grab a swisher. I began looking through the rows of alcohol. I liked Grey Goose but it was too expensive. Should we go dark and get some Henny or keep it light and get some apple Ciroc? I was lost in the selection when someone walked up on me, catching me off guard. My body got tense and I grabbed the counter. Instantaneously a few beads of sweat formed on my forehead. I wanted to scream out for Ricky but didn't want to give away that I wasn't alone. My mind was racing, I thought Eric was in jail.

"What's up?" he asked casually.

"Don't fucking talk to me."

"Fuck you. That's why I had her screaming y'all! She was hella scared, running from me." He started laughing.

"What type of man rolls up with a car full of people, and a gun, behind a stupid argument with a female? It's something really wrong with you."

The man behind the counter was silent.

Eric got angry and spit out "Whatever bitch!"

I was unaware Ricky walked to the front of the store. As the words left his mouth, Ricky rushed him grabbing him by his shirt. He lifted him halfway on the counter and moved one hand around his neck. Eric's entire face and demeanor changed. "It's good bra, it aint that serious." he quickly said. I grabbed Ricky and pulled him out of the store. Knowing that Eric likes to keep guns on him, I just wanted to get out of there. I was so grateful not to be alone in that situation. I didn't return to that store for almost a year. I learned over the years to avoid as much drama as I could. I had no interest in ever running into Eric again.

When I was 20, about 2 years into my relationship with Ricky, my mom and I were at a much better place. I had reached a point where I realized that I had to either cut our ties permanently or I had to forgive her and move on. The way I lashed out and treated her over the years was wrong. Yes, I was deeply hurt by a lot of my childhood, but at some point, we have to stop being a victim. Healing myself was my job and I did the work. I was not only improving my relationship with myself, but those seeds of positivity and growth were seeping into every area of my life. During this rebuilding period, she took Ricky and I on an all-expense-paid trip to New York. It would be a chance to travel together and enjoy each other's company. We enjoyed the trip as friends. It felt like we had begun to really choose each other for the first time in our lives. Ricky and I had such a wonderful time with her and Kenny. We explored Harlem, Brooklyn and Manhattan. We went to a Broadway show and spent the evenings exploring Times square. We hopped on and off the subway at random stops to see where we would end up. We took pictures at the Statue of Liberty and spent the evenings drinking and expressing our love for each other. We didn't have a lot of money to spend, but we had each other and that's all that was needed. The trip was amazing and a reminder we needed to get our lives together to do this more often.

At the beginning of the trip my mom gave me a book that was getting ready to change the course of my life. Life Rules by Yehuda Berg, literally shifted my view of the world. Our lives are shaped by our mindset and perspective, and at the time, both of mine needed an intense overhaul. I didn't finish it on the trip. However, the first few chapters alone planted seeds in my head and heart that were invaluable. It explained the importance of taking power over our lives. That we have control over our destiny no matter what happens to us. Often we cause our own situations while simultaneously blaming external people and circumstances. For example, imagine you are running late to a job interview. This interview is for your dream job, one you have been wanting for years. You are headed to the interview, there's a lot of traffic and a car is driving super slow in front of you. The tendency is often to be angry at the slow driver, mad at traffic and frustrated at every red light. The reality is you could have left earlier. If you were honest, the only person to be frustrated with is yourself. A deeper example can be taken from examining the end of a long-term relationship. Let's say your spouse cheated, you ended the relationship and you are angry. Of course, you would be hurt. But if you can step back and be honest, you will see that even in this situation, you played a part. Every relationship takes two. Maybe there was a lack of attention, communication or sex in the relationship. Possibly your attitude could use improvement. Maybe you showed up in the best way possible but ignored the warning signs right in front of you. Whatever it is, if you are truly honest with yourself, you will find some part you played in the demise of the relationship. The book Life Rules illustrates the importance of recognizing that in every moment, we have a choice. It also opened me up to the deep spirituality of Kabbalah. It revolutionized my thinking. I was determined to hold myself accountable for my own life. The subtitle was How to Turn Your Life From a Problem Into a Solution. It was exactly what I needed at that time. I was tired of the problems I was creating. I was exhausted. Tired of sleeping in my car, drained from my addictions and running out of the steam needed to keep living that fast lifestyle. I was ready to happen to life instead of it just happening to me. The book showed me I alone had control over my life. It was empowering. Soon, I would be forced to put these ideas into practice. I was running out of time to run wild. My life was getting ready to change in a way I wasn't expecting. I was about to face some tough lessons and life-changing experiences.

The wound is the place where the light enters you.

Rumi

Chapter 4- Change

Around the time that we got back from New York City, Ricky and I moved in with his cousins in West Oakland. I had no idea that I was preparing to go through a series of traumatizing events. We were in a large duplex that his cousin owned. We lived in the bottom unit with his two cousins and their girlfriends. It wasn't the newest home, and the area was rough, but it was a huge step up from my car. It was a large 3 bedroom, with a nice sized living room and kitchen. It was perfect as I was trying to shift my lifestyle. Long nights at side shows, a few hours of sleep in my car, then taking more ecstasy so I could go to work was wearing on me. Moving into a house was a blessing. A plus to his cousin's house was that it was in walking distance from my job at a local gas station. At the time I was working long shifts at the local Chevron. I was often clocking 50 hour work weeks. I chose to take graveyard shifts because I made an extra $1 per hour. The location was interesting. It was right between downtown and West Oakland. It sat directly off the freeway and was a stop for almost anyone going out on the weekends. People stopped to buy anything from snacks to condoms and swishers. Often 40-50 cars would fill the lot, dancing and having fun. Almost a mini side show on their way to the real thing. I never called the police so it could go on for hours before getting broken up. One evening it was the usual scene. The store portion of the gas station was locked after 10 pm. So, there was a line of people at the window, waiting for me to help them. Cars at every pump, with additional cars filling up every empty space. Most people were out of their vehicles, dancing to music and having fun. I looked up and noticed a beautiful Dodge Challenger. It was painted midnight green, sitting on 20 inch rims. You could hear his music from a block away, it sounded like he had a 15 inch speaker in the back. The man was sitting with his door open, rolling a blunt. From the side, another man ran up with a gun, someone I recognized - let's call him Al. From my vantage point I could see it all so clearly. Al grabbed the man by his legs and dragged him out of the car. The man was caught off guard and dropped his blunt, trying to grab onto the wheel to anchor himself. It was too late. He hit the pavement and they began to wrestle and fight. Al hopped in the driver seat. The owner of the car grabbed his shirt in an attempt to drag him back out. As they were fumbling around I saw Al reach for the gun. I knew he was going to shoot him. I pressed the button to the intercom, and even over the loud music, everyone in the lot could hear me. "Stooooooooppppppppppp!!!!!!!! Don't you dare shoot him!!!!" Al looked up and we made eye contact. "Don't you fucking dare!!!!!" It was as if I broke his trance. He paused before running off with the gun still in his hand. The owner of the car hopped back in, skirting away as fast as he could. I am so grateful I was the one working that night. In that area, things like that were common.

Late one evening, about 6 months into us living with Ricky's cousin, the house was quiet and everyone was asleep. We woke up suddenly to the sound of the front door being kicked in. If you've never heard the sound of a door being broken down, it's really really loud. It was around 3 am, and I was terrified and confused. Ricky yelled, "What the fuck!" as he leapt out of the bed. He ran to the door in boxers and a t-shirt to see who was breaking in. I was a few steps behind him. We were met by a swat team. They swarmed the front door with guns drawn, pointed at us, screaming for us to get on the ground. Our dog Hazel was barking like crazy, and they kept screaming to shut the dog up or they would kill her. We grabbed her, trying to quiet her down. The poor dog was so scared she defecated on herself. One police officer held a gun to the head of my cousin's girlfriend and ordered her to get on the ground. She was 6 months pregnant. She knelt down, trembling. Trying to obey without hurting the baby. We all laid down, face on the carpet, with our hands above our heads. Our request to see a search warrant was ignored. They brought in drug dogs to search the home and found nothing. The only drugs we had there was an eighth of weed, which is a relatively small amount. When the drug dog got close to the cabinet where the weed was kept, our cat leapt out and swatted him across the nose. It was like divine intervention. Plus, like I said, we were in the hood. Everyone was feisty, down to the animals. But more than that, our cat was our guardian angel that day. Even the police officer was like, "Dammmnnnn, your cat just fired on my dog." That was the first time since they burst into our house that we all started laughing, police included. While I don't think we would have gotten a charge for something so small, none of us wanted to find out. They even searched our cars. Usually mine would be littered with doobies, swishers and weed but thankfully I had cleaned it out a few days prior. We sat there for hours while this was happening, asking repeatedly to see the warrant. That request was repeatedly ignored. At the same time, they were raiding the upstairs portion of the duplex. There they found weed, cocaine, ecstasy, heroin and guns. They took our friend, the occupant, to jail. It turns out they had been watching him and building a case on him for months. It also turned out their warrant was for the upstairs unit only, not ours. They left us with an illegal search, broken front door and an oh well. Shortly after that, I told Ricky I couldn't live there anymore. It was too much for me. So, a month or two later, we moved to Richmond. We began living with his brother and sister-in-law. They were such a blessing to us. Richard and Juana opened their doors when we had nowhere else to go. Moving in with them was more than a roof over my head; it was home and a sense of family. We all lived together for several months. Despite how well we got along, eventually it was a lot to have two adult couples living in the same house. Richard and Juana moved out and got another home. That was something I really appreciated because we couldn't afford to move out. The house we were living in belonged to his grandmother, and she only charged us $300 a month. That was a huge blessing and made it worth the work. And it was a lot of work. It was used as storage and wasn't in the best condition. There was a spare bedroom we stuffed full of all the clothes, shoes, purses and random items she left behind. Most items were brand new, several still in the box. The quality or condition of the items was not a problem, it was the sheer quantity of stuff. The house was full and overflowing before we added anything of our own to the chaos. The physical condition of the house could use some love and tlc as well. There was a hole in the bathroom, right behind the toilet where the wall met the floor. From inside the bathroom, you could bend down and see the grass outside. I'm still not sure why we didn't grab some putty and close it up. I suppose there were enough other issues to tend to. The carpet was old, and the kitchen was older. We even found tons of mold in one of the bedrooms. We spent almost a week with bleach and rags scrubbing the walls and ceiling to clean it up. We were shocked to see that the walls we always thought were beige were originally white. Now, remember I had just spent a few years sleeping on buses and then in my car, so I was ok with it all. I would put in the work to make it as much of a home as possible. The one thing really hard for me was the mice. Even in the motels I lived in with my mom, there were never rodents. It was disgusting but still better than going back to sleeping in my car. In that house, I got used to things I never thought I could. The sound of mice scurrying around at night became normal. One day we were standing in the bathroom, smoking a blunt and a mouse literally ran through that little hole and hit my foot. I screamed so loud I think the mouse was more scared than I was. I'm telling you I saw things in that house I didn't even know were possible. I saw mice climb up curtains. I saw their bodies fit into the tiniest spaces. I cleaned and cleaned and cleaned. But because the house was literally falling apart, there was nothing I could do about the mice. Also, I was still taking ecstasy and smoking weed, which increased my tolerance to those conditions. Like how much shooting there was in our neighborhood. At the time we were living in Parchester village in Richmond, California. It was dangerous. There were shootings every day. Due to the way it was set up, it was difficult to get in and out of the neighborhood. There was one main entrance in and out. There was another small side exit, but it was barely used. Weekends were the most violent, and on evenings when we wanted to leave, we would literally wait for a break in the gunfire. If there was a long enough pause, we would run outside, hop in the car and hope for the best. Even for me, growing up in Oakland and Berkeley, this was a lot more than I was used to. However, my altered state of consciousness allowed me to live in situations I otherwise wouldn't have been able to.

My soul was itching for more. I was growing tired of the fast life. I was feeling off. I was tired all the time and less interested in getting high. I specifically remember one night riding around with Ricky doing our usual. We would take ecstasy, smoke, listen to music and talk for hours. On this particular night, I just wasn't in the mood. I took half of a pill and before I knew it, I was asleep. Ecstasy is an upper. It gives energy for hours. It's not something I ever went to sleep on. That evening was different. I was exhausted. Physically something had changed. A few days later, we took a pregnancy test and it was positive. My face flushed and tears came to my eyes. I had always wanted to be a mother. A second chance from the abortion I was still ashamed of. I still hadn't recovered from the pain and guilt of what I had done, but I was ready to make it right. I desperately wanted to create the mother/child relationship I always wanted. Deep down, I hoped having a child would heal the wounds I had masked over all these years. There was also another benefit. I had tried unsuccessfully to be sober for years. Every January, my New Years' resolution was to stop taking ecstasy and smoking weed. I never made it a full 24 hours without smoking. Every single year I failed. Being pregnant meant I would finally be clean. From the day I found out at 6 weeks, I was 100% sober. Finally.

They say if you want something, you have to fight for it. Nothing worth having comes easy. Our first trip to the doctor was a nightmare. I lay on the bed, excited as they hooked up the monitor. They couldn't find the heartbeat and told us we were probably having a miscarriage. My heart sank. I wanted this baby so badly. Ricky looked at me right at the moment I began to panic. Without a word, I was comforted and knew no matter what, everything would be all right. I pulled my shirt back down as he gathered our things. Without a word we left the hospital room. As we stood in the elevator waiting to leave, the last person to hop on was the ultrasound tech who had just turned our world upside down. It was silent for a few seconds until he looked over and recognized us. He must have seen how sad we looked because he said, "Don't worry! The baby might be fine. It may just be too early for a heartbeat. Come back in a week." A wave of relief ran through my body as Ricky and I exchanged a hopeful smile. Thank God he was right and our baby was ok.

The next hurdle came during a follow-up visit. My doctor sat me down for a serious discussion. A few months prior to getting pregnant, I went in for a yearly pap smear and found out I had abnormal cells. It was explained that left untreated they would lead to cervical cancer. The doctors were concerned enough they wanted to do a follow-up procedure, which they called LEEP. Essentially, they would be using a thin wire loop to cut off a small piece of cervical tissue for further examination. These results would confirm if the cells were precancerous, or if it was a false alarm. The day we went in, I had a bad feeling. When the doctor gave me my results, she informed me that the biopsy showed the beginning of cervical cancer. I was presented with two options. The first was to abort the baby and start treatment right away. The second option was to have the baby and hope for a vaginal delivery. The doctor explained that sometimes the trauma of pushing out a baby could take all the abnormal cells off my cervix, but it was a risk. It took me about two minutes to make my decision. I had promised myself that I wouldn't ever have another abortion. So, I decided to keep the baby in hopes that everything would be alright. It was the only choice for me, but it was emotionally difficult. I had struggled with anxiety and depression for years. Now having to worry about these cells developing into full-blown cancer during my pregnancy, was a weight heavier than any I had experienced in a while. The additional stress of approaching life sober, for the first time in years, was also difficult. I had wild mood swings that were hard to control. Ricky was often on the receiving end of my raging emotions. Sometimes we argued over the smallest things. One evening we were angry at each other for a reason I can't recall. After going back and forth for an hour, I retreated to our room. I plopped onto the bed, wanting nothing more than peace and sleep. Maybe 10 minutes after I drifted off, I was jolted awake by a loud noise. I shot straight up in the bed, looking around in confusion. Ricky had turned the tv up to the max volume. "You're an asshole!" I yelled out. He laughed as he left the room. Falling asleep wasn't the easiest because we were sleeping on a box spring with no mattress. I dozed back off before being jolted awake again. And then again. After the third unwanted wake up I was furious. My eyes were burning from exhaustion and I was desperate for sleep. "This is torture!" I screamed out to no response. A few minutes later I heard the front door open, and knew he was stepping outside to smoke. I threw on some clothes, grabbed my purse and snuck out the back door. Our 5 dogs ran up excitedly when I stepped outside. I looked over my shoulder hoping Ricky wouldn't hear. There was no side gate to our backyard, my only option was to climb the fence. I was 5 months pregnant. I placed a bucket next to my feet and used it to hoist my body up. Somehow, I managed to jump over while protecting my belly. I threw my purse over my shoulder and headed down the street. Before I could even get a block away, Ricky figured out I wasn't there and came running down the street. He grabbed me in a bear hug, pulling me back to the house. Exhausted, I lay down again. This time with no interruptions. Things like that can happen when you are young. Every couple needs a system to argue. A way to disagree that is healthy and effective for both parties.

Trying to figure that out takes time and effort. It was an additional pressure to the elephant in the room. I needed to upgrade my life. I was determined to bring my child into the best world I could provide and my expectations were high. I wanted my child to experience a stable home, with two loving parents. She or he would always have their own room, full of toys and books. They would be involved in activities and we would go on annual vacations. I wanted to be present in every way possible. But I was working 50 hours a week at a gas station, doing hair on the side and barely getting by financially. In order to make my desires a reality, some things would need to change. I wondered how I could put myself into a career in the shortest time possible. I looked into various options, concerned my record wouldn't make it easy. I decided on cosmetology school. I was 21 and hair was something I had been doing for years. I never saw it as a career, but knew I wanted flexible hours, good money and lots of time with my child. At this point, why not? It would be better than the gas station. Once I made the decision, I immediately put the wheels into motion. Focusing on new goals, helped me push the stress and fears out of my mind.

I had two options with cosmetology school. The first was going back to a junior college. That would be free and I would even get grant money. The downside was that it would take two years to complete. The other option was to go to a private cosmetology school. I could complete it under a year but would have to get loans to cover the $24,000 tuition. For me, the decision was obvious. I didn't have any time to waste. A few weeks later I hopped in a car my dad gave me and drove out to

Concord. It was an old car but I loved it. It was reliable and did the job. My previous car had broken down and I needed a way to get back and forth. I approached the unassuming large grey building with butterflies in my stomach. I was nervous and excited. A part of me knew this was the beginning of something different. Maybe it was because I had something to live for now, but I knew failing was not an option. I had dropped out of college and never gone back, but I promised myself that would not happen again. I walked into the best private cosmetology school I could find. Immediately the smell of burnt hair hit my nose. There was something about the white walls, rows of stations and girls busy over clients that got me excited. I sat down to talk to the director of admissions, consciously covering my stomach. I wanted to sign the contract without them knowing I was pregnant. I had no idea if it would matter, but I was nervous about anything stopping my plan. I left with the contract signed and a feeling that finally, my life would change. My child would not be born into a life of survival, we were going to thrive. I had a vision in mind and I was determined not to fail.

The months flew by while I was enrolled in Elite Progressive school of cosmetology. I was surrounded by good staff and great friends. The instructors had a wide range of skill sets and a wealth of knowledge to pass on to us. I have always loved to learn and this was no different. I enjoyed discovering the chemistry of color and the basics of cutting hair. They weren't the best with African-American hair, but luckily I had experience with that outside of school. I made a few great friends who would remain in my life long after graduation. There was

Alexie, the short spicy Filipino with no filter and a heart of gold. She tells it like it is, but always from a place of kindness and love. She married her high school sweetheart and had a relationship I always admired. There was also Danielle, a beautiful girl with long hair and blue eyes who I could sit and talk to for hours. Something about us clicked from day one. We started to get together outside of school. Then Brian was the hilarious flamboyant Hispanic man. He kept me laughing with inappropriate stories all day. Time flew while we ruined our doll heads with uneven color and choppy haircuts. Then there was my best friend, my dear Chanel. She was one of the few black women. We were pregnant at the same time until she lost the baby. She poured all her love into me. She would bring me snacks and rub my stomach every morning. Her kindness and compassion showed through the sarcastic humor that kept us all entertained. My circle of friends made a fun environment even better. One afternoon we had a guest hairstylist. She stood in front of the class and asked for a volunteer to get a cute bob style. I think we were all surprised when Catherine raised her hand. She was a shy, quiet girl. Rather mousey and the last you would expect to want a haircut from a stranger. She shared that she hadn't cut her hair in almost 10 years and was feeling adventurous. She went to the front of the class and settled in the chair. Our guest started hacking away. With every cut, my stomach got tighter. What is this lady doing? I glanced around the room, trying to gauge if I was the only one in full blown panic mode. Catherine was smiling, but she couldn't see her hair. Eventually she began to pick up on the energy in the room. 30 minutes later our guest, totally oblivious, smiled and spun her towards the mirror.

Catherine's forehead wrinkled up. Her face turned beet red and within moments her eyes got wet. Her lip trembled as a few tears slipped from her eyes. I'm not sure what part of that cut was supposed to be a bob, but it wasn't what any of us had in mind. A few strands of hair laid awkwardly on her forehead. At about an inch, it wasn't long or full enough to be a bang. The left side of her hair was considerably shorter than the right, but not short enough to look as if it was done on purpose. There were choppy layers in the top, with a random long piece resembling a duck tail in the back. It was edgy, different and the opposite of what she wanted. It felt like it belonged on the leader of a punk rock band, not a shy, quiet girl from Walnut Creek. We all smiled and thanked the guest. As soon as she left, we rushed Catherine as a group, all trying to comfort her. She looked at me "Natasha please, can you do a weave for me today? I've never had one, but I can't go home like this. I just can't." Two hours later her hair looked like it had never been cut, minus the short pieces in the front. Her hair stayed in a weave until it grew back out. Restoring her confidence filled me with so much joy and reaffirmed I was in the right career. I loved every aspect of school. It felt great to be sober, learning and growing. Even on the days when the elevator was broken, which was about 50% of the time, and we had to walk up 4 flights of stairs carrying all our tools, I was happy. Even on hot days (with no windows) and 30 girls practicing flat irons and curls, I was happy. I knew I was on the cusp of something great, and for that, I was thankful.

I was changing for the better but there was more work to do. I still had a little temper and was super emotional. However, I had learned dedication, perseverance and the importance of honoring your commitments and pushing through difficult situations. Around the halfway mark of school, I took a leave of absence to get married and have my daughter. Ricky and I went to the local courthouse to exchange our vows. It was a beautiful moment with only his cousin as our witness. A few days later, my grandmother hosted a party for us at her house. There was food, family and a cake. We didn't need a lot if we had each other. We were young, simple and in love. He still supported and accepted me as he had years earlier when we first met. That support was needed because I was approaching one of the hardest days of my life.

On June 19 I started cramping. Initially, it matched the worst period cramps I had ever had. Painful, but doable. My periods were always intensely heavy due to fibroids, so in that aspect, I was slightly prepared. By the middle of the night, I was waking up every 10 minutes with extremely sharp pains. They were shooting up my back, down into my thighs and were definitely more intense than earlier. They only lasted for a few seconds before they went away and I dozed back off. This continued throughout the night. Every contraction, I would gasp from the pain and Ricky would roll over to bear hug and squeeze my lower back until it passed. I was amazed that he knew to do counter pressure without us ever taking a birthing class. We were so in tune that he instinctively knew what to do. The pain continued through the morning, and by this point, I was getting tired and cranky. I tried to shift my focus by cleaning up around the house and finishing the last few braids in my hair. Later on that afternoon, I told Ricky I wanted to go to the store and I insisted on driving us. He kept asking if I was sure and saying maybe it wasn't a good idea. But when my mind is made up.... So, I got in the driver's seat and started the engine. As we pulled out of the driveway and approached the corner, I had another contraction. I immediately pulled into a ball letting go of the gas pedal. "Pull over. We are going to the hospital." I tried to put up a weak argument, but I knew it was time. We switched seats and about 30 minutes later we pulled into Kaiser. When the nurse checked my cervix, she said I was dilated to almost 7 centimeters and wouldn't be leaving until I had the baby. I was petrified. I planned to go all natural. They put me in the room and I focused on deep breathing techniques. The nurses kept reminding me I didn't have to endure that pain. I ignored them, determined to stick to the plan. At around the 30 hour mark the doctor came in. He explained that I needed an epidural. He said I would be too tired to push and needed some rest. I was too exhausted to fight. Once I agreed it was administered. They asked if a student could put it in. I refused and said she could watch. When the medicine took ahold it was such a relief and I was finally able to go to sleep. I missed the part about the medicine being self administered through a drip. I was unaware that I was supposed to keep clicking the button to release it. When it came time to push, a good portion of the epidural had worn off. It literally felt like my vagina was on fire. I pushed for so long they discussed a C-section. Determined to get her out naturally, I screamed and pushed as hard as I could. After 36 hours of labor, 45 minutes of pushing and the distinct sound of my vagina ripping she was here. My beautiful little Kamaya. I stared

104

at her while they sewed me up. I ended up with 6 stitches that were all worth it. She was this perfect little baby who looked like a doll. Beautiful caramel skin with these piercing dark eyes that stayed focused right on me. She had a curly head full of hair. I was in love. I enjoyed the following weeks home with her and wanted it to last so much longer. I could sit and stare at her for hours. She gave me a motivation I never had and I knew I had to return to school. But first there was something I needed to handle. Thanks to my daughter, when I returned to the hospital my pap smear was normal. All the cancerous cells came off during birth. Kamaya saved my life as soon as she arrived, quite honestly in more ways than one. For all of us, I was determined to move on to the next stage of my life. At the same time some of my old demons were creeping back.

I promised myself I wouldn't start back smoking. But a few months after I had Kamaya I was hanging out with some friends. They passed around a blunt and I decided to take a hit. I told myself it would only be once. Pretty soon I was smoking daily. Despite the set back, I returned to school focused and ready to get my license. One of the things I was most excited about when I returned was an amazing opportunity the school offered. It was actually what made me choose that school specifically. They were taking 20 students to London to study for a week at the Vidal Sassoon Master Academy. When it came time to sign up, I made sure my name was first on the list. I applied for financial aid to cover the cost and when the time came, I was ready. The day Ricky and Kamaya took me to the airport I was sad to leave them, but excited about the opportunity to train at one of the top academies in the world. The students and instructors flew out and traveled to the hotel as a group. Before we went to our rooms, the owner Manhal gave us the ground rules, the most important being to make sure you are in your room by 10 pm. We had one free day before the beginning of classes. It was made very clear that you could go wherever you want during the day, but if you missed curfew, you would be sent back to the states. Ok, easy peasy. So, a good friend and fellow student Ashley suggested going to Paris. A day trip to Paris sounded like a dream come true and I was super excited and ready to go. We were giddy with excitement on the train ride over. As we stepped out of the station, we were immediately hit with the strong, distinct scent of the city. Cigarettes, urine and an overpowering smell of garbage immediately took me off guard. The smells were unpleasant, but the city was gorgeous. The French inspired architecture was absolutely stunning, unlike anything I had ever seen. Huge buildings with the most intricate designs. I found myself in awe, even enthralled with the apartment buildings. There was stucco, brick and steeply pitched roofs. Other areas had a Roman feel with massive columns. We spent the first few hours riding a tour bus and exploring. Passing stores like Gucci, Chanel and Galeries Lafayette Haussmann. We hopped off and paused on street corners. Giggling while trying to pronounce the names. Rue de Rivoli, Avenue de Champs-Elysées et L'Esplanade des Invalides. I was mesmerized. We popped into tiny stores and gift shops to buy overpriced scarfs and trinkets. Together we tried sea salt galettes and chocolate eclairs from a local bakery. We stood on the bank of the River Seine, taking pictures on the way to the Eiffel Tower. We didn't have the time or money to eat at the restaurant in the Eiffel Tower, but we spent an hour exploring the area. Eventually we decided to get our return tickets to London. Early in fact, so we would have no concerns. Once we got to the counter, the woman told us the price of the ticket and Ashley's face dropped. She realized she didn't have enough money. My heart beat faster as I rummaged through my purse. After dumping all my money onto the counter, I discovered I had enough Euros for my ticket plus about half the cost of hers. In US dollars I had enough for both of us. I had no idea what to do. I didn't even own a credit card. Of course, we had shown up to the station 20 minutes before the last train went back; we didn't take into account that everything stopped running early on Sundays. I was so upset with Ashley, but I couldn't leave her behind. We literally begged the lady at the counter to take my money. I was desperate and in tears, which the employee must have found comical because a giggle escaped her lips. I had to take a deep breath and step outside, because I wanted to hop over the counter. I frantically looked for a money exchange. The 20 minutes flew by quickly and the last train departed. We were crushed. We knew we were rapidly running out of time to get back to London. We did not speak the language, had not found the people we encountered helpful or compassionate, and realized we had a very real problem. We looked into what other ways we could get back and a ferry seemed to be the most feasible option. With a little bit of difficulty we located the bus stop. It was starting to get cold, so we made up silly dances to keep us entertained. 45 minutes later the bus finally arrived. We happily clambered aboard, welcoming the heat and a chance to sit down. Rather quickly we arrived at the ferry station. Despite the circumstances, we were determined to laugh, have fun, and make the most out of the situation. One of the most valuable lessons I learned over the years is to enjoy life as much as possible- even when things are not going as planned. I had been through too much to panic over being stranded in Paris. All in all, it was still an amazing adventure. So we laughed and joked the whole way to the ferry. It was empty. We ran up to each counter to be sure, it was closed. It was getting close to 8 and our curfew was 10. For the first time that day, we called our parents and explained the situation. They looked into it and told us the only option left was to catch a plane. Unfortunately, they couldn't figure out what times any of the planes left. So, with no guarantee we headed to the airport, hoping to figure it out in person. On the way we called the owner and begged and pleaded to be allowed to miss curfew. After a long pause he agreed. But, if we weren't back to get on the bus with everyone else by 7:30 AM, we would be sent home. So, we caught the metro (which is the Paris rapid transit system) to the airport. Around this time the jokes were fewer in between. For the first time I was getting scared at the growing possibility of being sent home. Plus, it was late and dark in a city we did not know. The metro car was mostly empty. We sat in seats facing each other, glad to finally sit down and rest. A few minutes into the ride, the sliding doors that connect each train slid open and two men walked in. Each one, completely uninvited and unwelcome, took the empty seats right next to us. They started speaking to us in French and although we couldn't understand what they were saying we were very uncomfortable. Their vibe threw me off immediately. I could feel the energy radiating from them and I was scared. The man who sat next to Ashley slid his arm around her and she almost recoiled. My heart was beating fast and my mind was racing as the men continued to laugh, joke and be aggressive. Ashley was visibly uncomfortable but silent. A few moments later, the other man put his arm around me and his hand rested on my thigh. Without thinking, I reached in my purse and grabbed out my shears. Shears are expensive scissors we use to cut hair. They were almost $400, so I kept them on me to prevent them from getting lost or stolen. They were also the closest thing to a weapon I could find. I held them aggressively, pointing them towards the man next to me. At this point, both the men hopped up and stepped back. "BITCH I don't know what the fuck you're trying to do, but I will fuck you up!" I'm sure he didn't understand anything I was saying and the reality is I was terrified. But once he touched me, I knew I had to stand my ground. The man's face scrunched as he moved away from us. He mumbled words I didn't understand as they walked away. I thanked God both the men left. We sat back in relief but remained on guard until we made it to the airport. We arrived at Paris Beauvais-Tille. It was tiny and mostly empty, making it easy to rush and find an attendant. Our parents had to send us money to cover our tickets and we purchased the soonest available flight. It didn't leave until the next morning. But there was still hope because we were scheduled to arrive at 7 am. Our cut off to board the bus was 7:30. We planned on running off the plane, to a taxi and hopefully avoiding most of the Monday morning traffic. Despite our best attempts to make the most of the situation, we were tired, exhausted and hungry. The few people walking by were smoking cigarettes. It is a smell I detest. Despite the smell and discomfort, we tried to get the best sleep possible in the tiny plastic waiting chairs. When the morning came we anxiously boarded the smallest plane I've ever been on to head back to London. We sat there for several minutes. Anxious as the plane pulled off the runway 20 minutes late. It was a short bumpy ride. We landed, still hoping for a miracle that would get us to the bus in time. As we exited the plane, we broke into a full sprint from the ramp to a taxi. The driver seemed to take his time. We realized we wouldn't make the cutoff but could meet the bus at the academy in time to walk in with the rest of the students. We called and begged Manhal, but the answer was a firm no, we were to be sent home one day after we arrived in Europe. We approached the hotel at 7:45 am, 15 minutes too late. I was devastated as I finally accepted defeat. A few tears escaped. I wanted to be there so bad. I was one of a small handful of students who needed financial aid. I had worked so hard, taken out a loan and desperately wanted the educational experience being offered. I wondered silently if I should have left Ashley in Paris. But I knew it wasn't the right thing to do. I wished we would have been proactive and prepared for our return. We were responsible for what happened. We could have gone somewhere closer for our day trip, we could have purchased our return ticket in advance, we could have asked for help sooner. We could have stayed in London. It wasn't anyone's fault but our own. We gathered our things, exhausted and in tears, as we made our way back to the airport. I was massively disappointed. However, when I arrived back home, Ricky and Kamaya picked me up from the airport and I immediately felt like everything would be alright.

The comfort I received at home didn't change the embarrassment of returning to school. I had no choice, though. I had to swallow my pride, show back up and complete what I had started. It was a hard lesson learned. That even when you fail publicly, even when every piece of you wants to crawl under the covers and hide, you have to keep going. It didn't help that Ashley never returned to the school. We went through the experience together and I hoped we would support each other through graduation. Regardless of anyone else, I couldn't allow my embarrassment to stop me from my mission. Everyone at school knew what happened. So, when I went back to school, I made jokes about it and kept it pushing. I was getting close to graduation day and was eligible to intern once a week at a salon of my choice. The internship went so well that they hired me. It wasn't all smooth sailing and there were still more bumps along the road. However, I am grateful because God was preparing me. He was showing me how to keep going even when times get hard. I learned that when I really want something, I can't give up, no matter what. I got to see the magic that plays out when you focus on your goals, put in the work and manifest the ish out of them. Things were coming together.

Sometimes the past pops up in ways we don't expect. Pretty soon, I had graduated, completed my hours and was ready for the last step. Unfortunately, my application for the state board licensing exam got held up because of my record. I was told I might not get my license. I had a misdemeanor and 2 violations of probation, all of which were relatively recent. The last time I had set foot in a courtroom as a defendant I was pregnant. When I finished cosmetology school my daughter wasn't even one. I wasn't deterred, I had come way too far to give up. I knew in my spirit that this was another test, one which I would pass. I drove around the bay area and got all the documents I needed. Then I proceeded to write letters explaining every charge and how I had changed. After a few months, I was granted the right to take my test. Not without drama, the morning of, I overslept. After speeding the 45 min drive to the testing location, I ran inside as the last person to sign up, in the final 5 minutes before the doors were locked. With my mom by my side as my model, I took and passed the test and was licensed. Thank you God. I was learning some things about blessings and success. They come after the trials. They come after the hard work and disappointments. You don't learn and grow when everything is easy. It's the tough times that build character. It's in our hardest moments that we discover who we are and what we are capable of. These were lessons and skills years in the making. I had always been connected to God, but it was during my homeless days, walking around for hours cold, hungry and with nowhere to go, that he became my best friend. It was when I had no one else, that I realized he was all I needed. I learned to go within during the moments I wanted to give up. I used the pain as fuel to the fire to keep pushing. I learned the power of accountability and was ready to make something of myself. But I still had some bad habits, some of which were getting ready to resurface. I had some more pain to go through before I could reach my purpose.

Change is inevitable, transformation is by conscious choice.

Heather Ash Amara

Chapter 5- Salon Days

This is what I had been working towards for months. I was so proud of myself. What I didn't know was that if I wanted to live and operate at a higher level, God would have to shake my world upside down again. I was so happy to get hired at the salon I was interning at during school. It was a busy, fun, family-style, black salon. It was run by three sisters, none of whom actually did hair. They handled recruiting and hiring, organizing and day to day operations. They knew business. It was a perfect place to build a clientele. There were about 9 employees and 2 assistants. Half were stylists and the other half were barbers. We played music, cracked jokes and became like family. Jessie, Sunshine, Nake and Aisha became like sisters. The barbers, Chuck, James, Cleve and Patrick became family as well. They took me under their wings and taught me what I needed to know to expand my skills. I learned how to do some hair there. I also learned a lot about business. The importance of maintaining professionalism at all times, punctuality and how to manage a schedule. How to grow and retain a clientele base. I was good already, but I needed the experience to grow. We took classes together. We laughed and we cried together. We went to each other's weddings, baby showers and comforted one another during the separations and divorces. When a stylist had a birthday, the owners bought a cake and we all celebrated together. For the first time I actually enjoyed working on my birthday. We were a unit. I still remember the day we closed the salon and went to the Grand Lake theater to see This is It. The owners catered food and had drinks. We walked to the theater tipsy and happy. Working there was a beautiful experience.

One day Ricky and I were at home, not too long after I began working at the salon. We got a phone call that some drama was happening with his sister Tasha. We went over to her house to get filled in and to see what was going on. She had fallen out with an old friend and wanted to go by the house to grab her belongings. She called the girl and her mom, who said it was ok to come over. The whole situation felt messy, unnecessary and quite honestly like something I didn't want to be a part of. I had a feeling it would go left and repeatedly asked everyone to reconsider. We ended up over there anyway. When we pulled up, it was negative from the start. The girl's mom came out screaming, "It doesn't take all y'all bitches to come get this shit!" What a warm welcome. Before I knew it I replied, "Ok we here and what?" I honestly didn't mean to respond. The words came out of my mouth without thinking about it. Looking back, I wish they hadn't. The mother immediately walks in the street yelling, "Step to the street bitch step to the street!" She was definitely talking to me and my hopes of a peaceful exchange vanished. It's ironic because I am usually the one to calm a situation down. I actually don't mind someone feeling like they are punking me, as long as it means we can avoid a confrontation. So, I immediately went into my default mode of trying to diffuse the situation. "It's not that serious. All we want is to get the stuff". The woman had to be around 45. I was 23. I really did not want to fight. She must have sensed that, assumed I was scared, and it was adding fuel to the fire. The reality was I was nervous. There were so many people outside. I kept thinking, God, please don't let us fight, and if we do, please let me win. No one wants to get beat up in front of a crowd. Eventually, it got to where my back was literally against my car and she was in my face yelling. Tasha was between us, trying to break it up. The lady was definitely the aggressor, and Tasha was trying to calm her down. All of a sudden, I saw her hand pull back as she went to hit me. Tasha saw it as well and jumped out the way. At that point there was no more holding back. Everything moved quickly from there. She hit me and I clocked her right back. I'm not sure what she expected because she only hit me once. I was too angry to stop and we had switched with her back against the car. I had made it clear I didn't want to fight. I let her punk me. And that still wasn't enough. So, I wasn't going to stop after one hit. We were still fighting when I heard a man screaming behind us. "Bitch get off my mom!!!" I looked up to see her son running in our direction. Scared, I jumped back to avoid him hitting me, very aware a fight with a man was one I could not win. I looked around and it was chaos in the middle of the street. There were 3 fights going on at the same time. Every last one of us, ignorant and acting a fool. Until that point, the men stayed out of it. However,

116

when the son ran up to me, Ricky jumped out of the car. He is a 1st-degree black belt and with one hit the man dropped to the ground. Another lady ran outside, screaming and cussing. She was short and heavy. I'm slim and tall. Despite a 3 inch height advantage she was over double my size. Her hands were balled up in a fist, and it was clear she was ready to fight. I wasn't prepared to be hit first, again. So, I ran up and hit her in her face. We went at it until I heard, "It's getting hot out here. Hella people watching, we gotta go!" At this point the lady wasn't hitting me back. The fight was over. I turned and ran to the car. Adrenaline pumping as we drove off.

By the next day, I was over the whole thing. I wasn't happy about the way it escalated, but I was ready to move on. It wasn't something we thought much about for months. Until the day we got a sharp reminder. We found out Ricky had a warrant for his arrest. We were so confused. A warrant for what? After some investigation, we discovered the women lied to the police. They said he held a gun to the girl's head, hit her and stole her purse. After all that nonsense they started I was in shock. They were the aggressors. If anyone should have gone to the police, it's us. But the thought never crossed our minds. Not one of us mentioned calling the police. We certainly didn't think they would make that call. They were mad the fights didn't work out in their favor. I learned a really tough lesson that day. To avoid drama at all costs. That unless someone is a direct threat to me, I'm not getting involved. I should have followed my gut and stayed home. If I did that, I would have never been put in a position where I had to defend myself. All this mess could have been avoided. The consequences weren't worth it. Ricky went to jail for a year over that lie. These women showed up to court again and again. I kept thinking at some point, morals or a conscience would kick it and they would tell the truth. I was wrong. We were in a tough position. I did not have a lot of money and had to choose between a lawyer and bail. I chose a lawyer because we wanted to take it to trial. He was innocent and there were tons of witnesses. We were looking for vindication. I scheduled a meeting with the Alameda County District Attorney. I was honest about the fight and my involvement. None of it mattered. We learned a lot about the judicial system. We experienced first hand what happens to so many black men in prison. He sat in jail for almost a year, waiting for his case to go to trial. Going with the advice of his lawyer, he waved his right to a speedy trial. The purpose is to give time to gather evidence for a proper defense. The downside is they could keep him in jail indefinitely waiting for a trial. That is what happened. We showed up for his court dates, anxious to get it over with. Only to be disappointed when they were postponed every time. The reasons varied but the outcomes were the same. The judge would move his court date back 90 days, speaking as casually as if he was ordering a sandwich. Not realizing (or caring) that it was another 3 months Ricky would spend without his family or freedom. During this process he was offered several deals he refused to take. Why plead guilty to a crime when you're innocent? After over a year in jail, approaching 400 days incarcerated, we figured out the answer to that question. Eventually you lose faith in the judicial system. To spend a year waiting for a trial is a gross injustice. You get desperate, feeling like it will never end. Then they continue to offer plea deals, which becomes more and more tempting to take. One day he finally got an offer too good to pass. He would get out the following week. The other option was to keep waiting for a trial that kept being postponed. He gave up and took a charge for something he didn't do. He walked out of jail the following week having lost so much. A year of his life, the chance to prove his innocence and a sense of justice were all gone. When he first went to jail, I kept saying he's innocent! I told everyone who would listen, convinced the truth matters. A friend told me innocence is irrelevant. By the time this situation was over, I realized in this case it was true.

I was very hesitant to bring up this story. I felt anxiety as every word came out. It is a closed chapter I had no interest in opening. It is something we have all moved past. But this is my story and Ricky going to jail affected the rest of our lives. I forgive them and I hope they forgive me for my part. I will never bring up names but the lies they told had lasting ramifications. Because of that, this story had to be shared. By the time Ricky was released, so much had changed. I had worked so hard to be there for him. I paid for his lawyer, food and phone calls. I sent him books to take his mind off of reality. I visited every single week, the entire time he was incarcerated. It was agonizing for him, but it was extraordinarily difficult for me as well. A police officer dragged him into a corner without a camera, beating him up. As a black belt he could have fought back and hurt that man, but he probably would have been killed. So instead, he had to sit there and take it. And I had to listen to what happened. It hurt us both. I worked my ass off at the salon to provide for myself, our daughter and him.

Despite that, during this time I changed. My expectations and mindset shifted. By the time he got out we no longer fit like the puzzle pieces we once were. Our vibe changed, arguments started and we drifted apart. We were so used to it being us against the world. We didn't know how to handle it being us against each other. Within a few months of him coming home we split up. I was sad, depressed and unsure of my decision. I had chosen to leave, yet I was indecisive. Sometimes, I wanted to work it out. Sometimes, he wanted to work it out. It never happened at the same time. At our first break up it was over.

Divorce is a loss and there was so much grief. Yet through it all I had total faith. Everything happens for a reason and God has my back. There was a path, even if I couldn't see it. I stayed busy because it hurt more when I was still. Emotions could creep in at any time. There were moments I was over a client and it would take over. I would excuse myself, running to the bathroom to hide my tears. Then splashing my face with water and reappearing with a smile. Luckily those were the rare occasions. Most days work helped me forget. Within six months of our separation, I literally doubled my income. Actively turning my pain into something positive. Money was good, but I needed a plan to work through the emotions. I couldn't keep avoiding them. First thing every morning I put on a sermon. I went to bed every night doing the same thing. I had CDs from my church that helped me through my most difficult moments. My favorite was entitled I Want Me Back. I listened to it so many times it was starting to skip. Then one day a lady came in to get her hair done. She seemed sad and

120

depressed, then shared she was also going through a divorce. I let her borrow my sermon, a copy I had for over 5 years. She walked back into the salon a week later looking lighter. She listened to the whole sermon that day, and several times since. She played it in her car leaving the salon, then found herself driving around without a destination, enthralled in the words. She handed it back carefully and we hugged. There was power in those words that got me through. I focused on God, my spirituality and my daughter. I kept her during the week and loved every minute. We enjoyed cooking, playing and spending time together. We read books, went on movie dates and got henna tattoos. I put her in ballet, then tap and Tae Kwon Do. She even tried trapeze. I was at every practice and show. I put her in cheerleading and was the team mom. I loved making gifts for the team, everything from custom jackets to bedazzled water bottles. We spent afternoons at bookstores, continuing a tradition I enjoyed with my own mom as a child. As with anyone, I'm sure I could have been better. More patient, more relaxed. However, I had her back. In every way, every time. I tried my best to create the mother-daughter relationship I always wanted.

In alignment with staying busy, I also re-enrolled in school. I was building a clientele at work and studying in between clients. There were stacks of books in my station at all times. Clients laughed when I reached for products stored on top of a Statistics book. It was a running joke in the salon, but it was all love. I was on my own unique path. Then the day came. I finally graduated with my AA in social science. Despite it not being a four-year degree, I felt an immense amount of pride. I proved so much to myself. Graduating and walking the stage gave me so much confidence. It was my first time crossing a stage since middle school. I did it as a single mother while working full time. It wasn't easy but I stopped making excuses and pushed through. God was blessing me through the storm, and it was amazing.

The salon I was at was a commission salon. Meaning they got a percentage of every client I did. It was expensive, but it worked. They provided the clients, I did the work and we split the money. It was a win-win. Sometimes I would also take clients at home so I would get the full amount of the service. One day after work, I headed to a client's home. When I pulled up, Sherita met me with a big smile. She bounced up to the gate and let me in, ready to share the best news I had heard in a while. She had a new job as an apartment manager. I glanced around the gated community of townhouses with a smile. "If you know anyone who needs a place to stay, we are renting." I hadn't told her Ricky and I had split, but it was the perfect time to share the news. I let it all out. That it was over. I had been sleeping at my dad's, with Kamaya, for the last 2 months. She rubbed my shoulder and walked me into a beautiful home. It was an impressive upstairs/downstairs condo. Large and clean with two bedrooms and two bathrooms. A nice sized living room and new kitchen. There was even a small patio in the back. The perfect space to do clients and a gorgeous first home for me and Kamaya. I wanted it. My mind was already turning with ideas on how to decorate. It was incredibly well priced and was a step up from anywhere I ever lived. God clearly had a plan. It felt like water in the desert. An umbrella in the rain. When something is meant for us, it is for us. I knew this was meant for me. I didn't have much money saved and normally I wouldn't be bold enough to ask for an exception. Here I had no hesitation. God's gift was clear. I asked if I could break up the deposit. I wanted to attach it to my monthly rent. I had no check stubs or credit and a limited work history. Despite all that, I was not deterred. Thankfully neither was Sherita. She had known me for years. She said she knew how hard I worked and would try to get me in. When the owner agreed, my gratitude went beyond a place to stay. It brought me closer to God and reminded me of some major lessons. How he takes what seem to be the worst situations, then uses them to propel us to where we are supposed to be. We don't make changes when we're comfortable. When we are pushed to be better, we can exceed our wildest expectations.

The blessings didn't stop with a beautiful townhouse. They kept coming as moving day quickly approached. I drove to a friend's house to buy some weed, figuring a few blunts would get me through the day. When I pulled up, I was surprised at the moving truck in front. Turns out he found out less than 24 hours prior that he had to move. After talking for a few minutes, he offered to let me use the truck and help me move all my stuff. On top of that, he gave me a gorgeous original painting by Amed Ali (which we later found out was worth over $1,000). The painting still hangs in my living room, over 10 years later. And the blessings continued. One afternoon I walked into a local used furniture store. I needed a couch for the living room and a kitchen table with chairs. I had high hopes but a small budget. Within a few minutes I found 2 couches. They didn't match, but at least they were the same color. Towards the back of the store there was a beautiful wooden table. My total, including delivery, was under $120. I couldn't believe my luck and was so excited to share the news. When I told one of the owners at the salon, she literally cried. That level of support was a reminder of all the blessings through the storm.

One more incident shocked me. One of my coworkers, Jessie, became like a sister. I could call her for literally anything. We talked, laughed and cried together. She was there for me through the good and bad. When I didn't want to dress up alone on Halloween, she put on butterfly wings and showed up early. If I lost my temper, she was ready to fight. When I called her in tears, she was my comfort. She was by my side no questions asked. There was no judgment on either end. One day we were driving. I was sharing how God and the universe had blessed me with every single thing I needed. "Girl, even down to the painting for the wall! All I need now is some nails." We laughed. "Tash, pull over so I can smoke this cigarette. I know you hate the smell". She rolled her eyes and we laughed again as I stopped in front of a random laundry mat. A few minutes later I looked up trying to figure out what she was doing. She took a few steps then bent down to grab something off the pavement. Took another step and grabbed something else. My excitement built as she walked back towards the car. She sat in the passenger seat with her hands cupped. I looked over and saw about 8 nails. They weren't just any nails, though. They were the nails with hooks attached, the ones made specifically to hang a painting on the wall.

124

My faith was at an all-time high. That's the beauty of pain and tough times. It gives us lessons, creates strength and prepares us for what's next. As we overcome the struggles, we strengthen our faith. Whether you believe in God, Karma or energy, life has a way of reassuring us. Things weren't perfect. The divorce was hard and I felt alone. Yet I knew things would be ok. Despite my assurance I had another struggle, I had fallen back into addiction. After the divorce, I started taking ecstasy again. At first, it was a weekend thing, something I did when I didn't have Kamaya. Pretty soon, it was a daily habit. I was a functioning addict and I rationalized a lot. I told myself that since I had a successful career, a stable home environment and was always there for my daughter "my addiction wasn't that bad". I was the primary parent, so I must be doing alright. All justifications that didn't change the truth, one too painful for me to acknowledge at the time. I could not be the mother I wanted to be when I was on drugs. Being her mom was my number one priority, but it wasn't enough to keep me clean. Sobriety is only maintained when you do it for you. I loved Kamaya. But I needed to love me enough to stop.

One day I was coming off the freeway, headed to the salon. Ironically off the same exit where the car almost t-boned us years before. It was a super busy area, and I sat in a long line of cars. I was in the second lane, several cars back from the crosswalk. A homeless man was walking slowly across the street. He looked tired and dragged down by life. Like the weight of the world was on his shoulders. His clothes held layers of dirt and grime. He was in a mixture of outfits, piled on top of each other to keep him warm. A plaid ripped top, above a red sweater, on top of other items I couldn't make out. A feeling of despair radiated from him. I said a quick prayer asking God to send him help. As soon as the words formulated in my mind, the man stopped dead in his tracks. He looked directly at my car and changed direction. He didn't make eye contact, but out of all the cars it was clear he was walking to me. My heart pounded as he approached my window. I rolled it down and handed him $5. He grabbed the money and shuffled slowly away. I didn't give him a huge amount and we didn't speak, but it was one of the most powerful experiences I have ever had. It was God telling me not to ask others to do what I can do myself. While I was asking for someone else to help him, it was I who was supposed to do the work. Too often, we pass off responsibilities to other people. We leave it up to someone else to step in, stand up or lend a hand. Maybe no one ever does. We sidestep what we can so easily do ourselves. Help those around us. It was a reminder of how deeply we are all connected. It's a human thread that joins us regardless of color, religion, education or status in life.

Your time is limited, so don't waste it living someone else's life. Don't be trapped by dogma. Which is living with the result of other people's thinking. Don't let the noise of others' opinions drown out your own inner voice. And most important, have the courage to follow your heart and intuition. They somehow already know what you truly want to become. Everything else is secondary.

-Steve Jobs

Chapter 6- A Dangerous Love

I was learning and growing, but the hard lessons were nowhere near over. I was about to get myself into one of the scariest situations of my life. A period so crazy I still look back and thank God we both made it through all right. The period directly after a divorce is usually rocky. The same was true for Ricky and I. We went through months of barely getting along. Pick ups and drop offs had to be done through my mother. For a while we couldn't stand to look at each other. There was too much pain, hurt and disappointment on both ends. But we pushed through for Kamaya. We knew we needed to heal and move on for her sake. I listened to daily sermons, which helped me dramatically. Then one day a friend invited me to go somewhere. I had no idea what I was getting into. He just told me there was an amazing lady, who worked with releasing energy. I had a lot to let go of, so I went. We showed up to a small building and walked in a mostly empty room. There were about 8 people, including my friend and I. We sat in hard wooden chairs, formed in a half circle, all facing the woman. I had no idea what to expect. She asked us to share why we were there, one by one. I felt flushed and uncomfortable, not expecting to share my private feelings with a group of strangers. But I wanted help and had nothing to lose. After the last person went, she instructed us to close our eyes and focus on the issue. I sat for a few minutes, concentrating on Ricky. At first I felt irritation, thinking of all we had been arguing about. Suddenly there was an intense energy. It felt as if a room full of people were staring at me. I cracked open one eye, peeking to see if she was looking in my direction. She was facing straight forward, eyes closed. I shut my eye back, took a deep breath and kept concentrating. Even without visual confirmation, I sensed she was focusing on me. There was a tingle throughout my body and a rush of emotions so strong I was caught off guard. I felt a shove on my shoulders and my body jolted back as my eyes flew open. Everyone else looked peaceful and no one was around me, so I closed my eyes again. This time I was nervous, confused and unsure of what to expect. Moments later I felt a huge ball of energy come directly out of my stomach, up my throat and release from my body. It was the most amazing thing I ever felt, followed by nothing. The feelings and emotions were gone, except a slight bewilderment. I leaned back in the chair and yawned, suddenly exhausted. My mind was turning in awe and confusion. At the end of the evening, as we stepped out the doors of the center, I grabbed his arm "What was that?" Reiki. When I got home I spent an hour on google searches, fascinated by what I found. Our bodies hold energy. Every conversation, argument and experience leaves something behind. Over time it can weigh us down. Heavy emotional experiences can be sensed physically as well. It's like the phrase, carrying a weight on your shoulders. Emotional baggage is a real thing. And if you don't find a positive release it can lead to disease, both mental and physical. Reiki masters know how to harness energy. She was able to move all these negative emotions, literally out of my body. I felt lighter, happy and content. Things I was upset about no longer bothered me. It wasn't a magic solution, but it was life changing. I was able to interact with Ricky from a totally different place going forward. I was reminded that we were both human. We didn't agree but that's ok. We were each on our own path, moving through life the best way we knew how. Blame was a wasted emotion, instead it was time to let go. So, after a period of ups and downs, we started to find our rhythm. Within about 8 months, things had smoothed out and we were back to getting along. The divorce was close to being final, and I think we were both ok with how things were. We were working on rebuilding as friends and co-parents. Since being friends was always our strong suit, we shifted into that space quite well. Kamaya was all that mattered and we wanted her to see a positive relationship between us.

As I healed, I became interested in seriously dating again. I began to talk to people here and there, but it was nothing serious. One day I was at the salon laughing and chatting with a client. I felt someone staring and looked up to see this fine chocolate man. He was talking to one of the barbers but his attention was on me. I immediately blushed as I pretended not to see him staring. This wasn't his first time in the salon. In fact, I always noticed when he came in. He was 6'4, chocolate and hard to miss. His features reminded me of Denzel Washington. I could barely look him in the face without blushing and turning red. This was the first time I think he noticed me. He walked up to me and asked for my number. I looked down at my client, avoiding eye contact. Then softly said ok. The rest of the day, I kept checking my phone, waiting for him to call.

We ignore what we aren't ready to face. We pretend we don't see things that aren't conducive to what we want. Honestly, on the first date, I knew it would not work. We were talking and getting to know each other when he told me he wasn't interested in a relationship. I smiled, said it was nice to meet you and hopped out of the car. He looked surprised and asked for a chance to explain. I sat back down when I should have kept going. I like relationships, casual dating isn't for me. Any man not open to building a future was a waste of time. Plus, I've always been a sucker for love. I'm reserved when I first meet someone. Male or female. Because I know that if I let my guard down and get my emotions involved, then I am all in. That's why his statement was an immediate red flag. People tell us what they want and who they are. But we ignore that for what we want to see. I knew in the end it would not go anywhere. But I wanted to believe him. He explained he was open to a relationship, just not in a rush to find it. Despite my better judgement I decided to give it a try.

We vibed. We talked for hours about vegetarianism, the plight of the black community, health, wellness and spiritual growth. We strategized on ways we could come together and uplift ourselves and our community. He took me to bookstores and out to eat at Eritrean restaurants. We had fun. I started to fall in love when he introduced me to Assata Shakur. We were in a small shop, browsing around. There was one tiny bookshelf and there sat her book. I never heard of her. He assured me I would love it. It ended up changing my life. I have always found transformation through books. Life's too short to learn all lessons through direct experience. Sometimes we have to learn through other people's stories and hers has a lot to teach. She was a black activist and a part of the Black Panther Party. As with anyone fighting for black rights in America, she was considered a threat. The FBI went undercover, infiltrating and destroying the BPP. Ironic, especially when the KKK is still alive and well. One evening while driving on the New Jersey turnpike, the car she was in was stopped. A New Jersey state trooper shot her with her hands in the air, then sat there waiting for her to die. She was still conscious while the paramedics argued they had to take her to the hospital, for fear of losing their jobs. She survived and was charged on multiple false charges, acquitted on three. After being wrongfully convicted she was sent to a predominately white prison, probably in hopes she would be murdered. She was broken out of jail and escaped to Cuba, where she still lives as a political refugee. Now these statements are according to her, google has slightly different versions. I believe Assata. Her story was amazing, with so much wisdom woven through. She didn't smoke or drink in an effort to keep her mind clear. She read hundreds of books and had a deep desire for fairness and equity. She is strong, intelligent and a fighter. I admired her story and Lawrence for introducing me to it. From there on I looked at him differently.

Books are to me, what makeup is to some. I collect them. I still have all my books from childhood. The Secret Garden, Chronicles of Narnia, Eric Jerome Dickey and so on. Books like Black Girl Lost and Souls of Black Folks by W.E. DuBois has moved with me from home to home. It has been very rare for me to date someone who likes to read as much as I do. I never had anyone introduce me to books that changed my life. Our conversations and experiences were eye-opening for me. We aligned on so many levels. We both were totally against fast food. I would literally go hungry before eating Wendy's or Taco Bell. Fast food was a non negotiable, somewhere I've never taken my kids. Neither of us were big on meat or dairy. I hadn't eaten pork, beef or milk for years. We preferred natural remedies and could easily spend an afternoon in a health food store. We were excited about getting herbs and supplements to add to our collections. We loved to hike, walk and enjoy nature. A perfect off day was spent exploring trails throughout the Bay Area. We enjoyed concerts and going out dancing, despite having slightly different tastes in music. It was to be expected since he was 15 years older. When we went out he was focused on me, I didn't even see him looking at other women. I get territorial so that's something I notice and can be an instant deal breaker. Then there was the sex. He was experienced and had no problem taking control. He picked me up, bent me over and hit all the right spots. I melted. It was as sensual as if from a woman. We both had a high sex drive and couldn't get enough of each other. He would pick me up on every lunch break and take me out every evening. Often, we would sneak off to have sex. We were intimate in the car, the woods on a hike and every corner of our homes. I was falling for him fast. I introduced him to my daughter, met his little girl and we were all getting along. I was all in. I felt like I had met the man I might spend the rest of my life with, albeit rather quickly after my divorce. We were connected intellectually and emotionally. There was so much fire and passion physically. Much to my happiness and surprise, we eventually entered an exclusive relationship. Despite that, I had a constant nagging feeling. Something wasn't quite right. One day he went to the bathroom and I seized the opportunity to look through his phone. The messages in his phone were all to other women. Name after name. Brandi, Courtney, Whitney, Patti, Jasmine, Alicia, Pam, Terri. The list went on and on. Multiple conversations, inappropriate pictures and plans to meet up for dates. My heart dropped. My feelings were so incredibly hurt. I was surprised despite the warning signs. There were big ones I had chosen to ignore because I had already fallen in love. Like the fact that he slept with his phone. Who does that? Like literally sleeping with it under him. Even when he accidently left it out there was a lock on it. The second red flag was that his ringer was always on silent. He was also weirdly obsessed with the idea that I was cheating, which I wasn't. It was not the occasional cute jealous moment. It went far beyond anything I had ever experienced, and I had experienced a lot. I had my run ins with unstable men, and somehow rationalized the behavior. I didn't know Lawrence was going to scare me more than any other man so far.

He was around me almost every waking moment. Even when I was at work he popped up several times a day. I thought it was because he missed me. I thought it was cute. But soon I realized it was a control issue and he wanted to know where I was at all times. My phone was always unlocked, so he could go through it whenever he wanted. I hoped he would realize I had nothing to hide. Yet he insisted I was cheating. It quickly moved from verbal accusations to odd behavior. I caught him going through my phone when I walked back in the room. I walked in on him rummaging through the drawers in my home. Frequent invasions of privacy. It continued to escalate rapidly. There were several times I caught him peeking in through my windows. I would step outside to smoke or take out the garbage and catch him right outside my house, always acting as if he was just about to call. Once I was walking to the laundry mat next door and Kamaya yelled out "Hi Lawrence!" I looked up to see him hiding behind a clothing donation box. He stepped out as if everything was normal. He was always trying to catch me doing something I wasn't doing. I had been with jealous men but he was taking it to a whole new level. Once the apartment manager knocked on my door and asked me to step outside. He told me he saw Lawrence hop the gate to get into our complex. He made it clear that if he saw him do that again, he would call the police. It was crazy, even more so because it was a tiny side gate I didn't even know was there. Another time I was washing dishes and cleaning up the kitchen. I glanced outside on my small patio. The area was surrounded by trees and therefore always covered in leaves I never had time to sweep. I noticed a path cleared from the edge of the fence, right up to my back window. The leaves were piled so high on either side, that it was impossible for the path to have occurred naturally. I knew it was Lawrence creating the perfect way to walk up undetected. Yet another time, I was watching TV and noticed small holes in my curtains. It was odd. How does something hanging up get a hole in it? I dismissed the thought until a few months later. During an argument he admitted to cutting holes in the curtains so he could see in. A possibility that never crossed my mind.

All that was just the beginning. Suddenly I was in too deep. Scared to try and get out. His behavior was shocking and I didn't know what he was capable of. My past experiences proved you never know what a person may do. He repeatedly broke into my home. Sometimes when I was there and I believe a few times when I was gone. One afternoon I came home from work. I was tired and my body was on autopilot. I stepped up to the door, keys in hand. Gasping as I noticed that my front door sat slightly ajar. My heart started pounding and I felt dizzy. Trembling, I pushed open the door, instantly aware someone had been in my home. I stepped into the living room. Couch cushions were overturned, magazines were on the floor and the table was pushed out of place. I gripped my keys tightly as I stepped into the kitchen. Every cabinet was sitting wide open with pans and food scattered on the floor. What could they be looking for, money stashed in a sugar jar? It was ridiculous. I turned and slowly made my way up the stairs, leaving the front door wide open in case I needed to run. At the top of the stairs I peeked into Kamaya's room. Her dresser drawers were open and there were toys everywhere. I took a few more steps down the hall before turning into my room. That's where the real chaos was. My clothes were ripped off the hangers and tossed out of my closet, every drawer was wide open and even my mattress was flipped over. I crumpled to the floor and cried. I felt angry, violated, confused and scared. I allowed myself 10 minutes of self pity before jumping into action. I bent down, slowly gathering clothes in a pile to be washed. Then I headed to my daughter's room to rearrange the mess. The rest of my evening was spent cleaning my house. In the process I took a mental inventory of my belongings. The only valuable thing taken was my wedding ring. That was the first time it crossed my mind that it might be him. When I looked closer, the whole thing felt staged.

If we got into an argument where I refused to let him in my house, he would calmly jimmy the window until he got it open. Then come inside and sit down as if nothing happened. I couldn't physically remove him, so he would stay as long as he pleased. It left me paranoid. At night I would wake up at any little noise, unsure if he was breaking in. In fact it was easier to just have him there, at least then I wasn't constantly looking over my shoulder. I never gave him a key but he still had full access. Within a few months, I learned to do a full sweep when I got home. Checking every window, door and closet became my normal routine. Only after that would I shut and lock my front door. A shift happens when your privacy is repeatedly violated. I simply never felt safe. One Friday evening Lawrence and I were cooking and hanging out. I mentioned to him that a friend wanted to stop by. The energy immediately shifted. He got quiet and walked out the room. He planned on spending the night but suddenly announced he was leaving. I didn't know why and wasn't in the mood to figure it out. I gave him a hug and kiss, knowing he would return whenever he felt like it. About 30 minutes later there was a knock at my door,

Gabby had arrived. We spent an hour laughing, drinking and talking before we started hearing a weird noise. It sounded like someone fumbling with a window upstairs and it was coming from my daughter's bedroom. My friend jumped up and said she wanted to leave. I begged her not to go until I went upstairs to check it out. It was the weekend so thankfully Kamaya wasn't there. I slowly crept upstairs. The double doors to her room were wide open, making it easy to see inside. The window, which I made sure was locked, was now halfway open. A man was climbing through. All I could see was the top of his head and shoulders. We both screamed, and I sprinted past her room to grab my gun. The man jolted back and took off running, without me ever getting a look at his face. I ran into her room, gun in hand. I swung open her back door, which led to a balcony. Panting I whipped my head back and forth, there was no sign of the intruder. I slammed the door, triple checking the lock before relocking the window. Immediately I called Lawrence hysterically crying and begging him to come back. Less than 10 minutes later he was at my door. When he walked in, something was off. There were beads of sweat on his forehead and his shirt felt damp. He sat on the opposite couch and kept fidgeting with his shirt. It just didn't feel right. I had a nagging feeling in my gut. Although I only saw the top of the intruder's head, I felt it in my spirit it was him. But that didn't make sense. Why would you do that? Why would you leave voluntarily and then try to break in? My mind was running as I tried to talk myself out of that possibility. I wasn't sure which was scarier, it being a stranger or him. People break in during the day to steal your belongings. People break in at night to hurt you. Plus, the intruder came in through my baby's room. That created thoughts too terrible to mention. For the next two days I slept on my couch and he stayed with me. I was having nightmares and terrified to bring Kamaya back on Monday. One night he turned to me and confessed it was him. He was the intruder. I didn't understand why. He claimed to have thought I was messing around with the girl. Then decided to leave and sneak back to check on us. When he finally admitted it was him, he expressed guilt over the level of fear and anxiety I was experiencing. He thought he was alleviating my concerns with his confession. Instead my worries hit an all-time high. I had no idea how any of that was logical to him. My mind was racing as I wondered, what have I gotten myself into?

In between the craziness there were good moments. We enjoyed time together but were constantly fighting and making up. One night we got into a huge argument about him cheating, yet again. A client saw him out one evening in a club. He was dancing and talking with multiple women. She witnessed him getting a few numbers. I was embarrassed and humiliated. You never want that kind of news about your spouse. At some point in the argument he screamed he was leaving. I heard the front door slam and didn't bother to get up. I laid in my bed and cried. When I was out of tears I went to my default, weed. I felt around for a lighter in the sheets, under the bed and on the dresser. Coming up empty, I headed downstairs to light it on the stove. I stood in the kitchen and took a few hits of the blunt. I let out a huge breath before leaning against the wall. The weed always relaxed me. I began to head back upstairs, content with a solo movie night. Right before I made it to the bottom of the stairs, Lawrence stepped out of the downstairs closet. I screamed and dropped the blunt. "What the fuck are you doing?!" He laughed and said he decided not to leave. Tears filled my eyes as we walked back upstairs.

One evening I heard a familiar fumbling at my living room window. By this point, it was a noise I recognized and was tired of. I thought about calling the police but quickly disregarded the notion. Calling the police for help could end with me dead or in jail. In my previous experiences they weren't usually an ally, even when I was asking for help. So instead, I ran to grab my gun, planning on scaring him off. I stood halfway up my stairs, facing the window and front door, waiting for him to get in. Minutes later he was climbing through my front window. I yelled out multiple times, "Leave! Get the fuck out! I have a gun and I'm tired of this shit! I'm not playing with you." Instead of leaving, he sprinted towards me. The look in his eyes terrified me. He lunged up the stairs and we wrestled as we fought over the gun. All of a sudden, I heard a loud bang. I dropped the gun and started crying, realizing it went off. I looked at Lawrence, he was sweaty but fine. I frantically tried to figure out where the bullet went. I glanced to the right and spotted a tiny hole in the wall. My heart sank as I realized I accidentally shot a bullet into my neighbors' wall. She lived there with her young son. I dropped to my knees, praying that no one was hit. Thank God everyone was ok. At that moment, I knew our relationship had to end. Someone could have lost their life and we were both at fault. Staying together would lead to death, jail or misery. I couldn't get away yet, but I was plotting. What I did immediately was get rid of the gun. I didn't want any chance of something like that happening again.

The final straw happened on the eve of my 25 birthday. We were on my balcony talking. You could tell he was in one of his moods. He was being rude and the conversation was tense. I was doing my best to ignore it and get along. All I wanted was a good birthday. During the time we were together, I had brought in a lot of holidays alone because he started an argument so he could go out in peace. I didn't want my 25th to end up the same way. I turned to him.

"Please, let's just get along."

"Don't worry. You can stop acting like a bitch. I'm going to spend time with you on your birthday."

I was silent. We had argued, fought and had crazy times. He was often demeaning, throwing personal things in my face. He didn't hesitate to talk down on me for smoking weed, the music I listened to or choices I made. My words could also be sharp and cruel. But what he didn't do was call me out my name. That is a non-negotiable for me. The ultimate disrespect. As soon as those words left his mouth, I knew it was over. There were times when I was so angry I would throw pots and pans at him, sometimes filled with hot food. This time I wasn't mad, instead I finally accepted we had to end. All the craziness we experienced and that was my final straw. Quite often that's how it happens. A person takes so much, until one day they are fed up. I chose not to spend my 25 birthday with him. The relationship was over. Still, instead of a clean break, there was a grey period that dragged on for months.

A few months later I met someone I really liked. At the time, Lawrence and I still talked occasionally. I told him during one conversation he had to stop calling me. I explained the situation. It wouldn't be fair to anyone involved if Lawrence and I kept talking. He said ok and that he understood. He didn't call after that and I was feeling good, free from the toxic relationship we both played a part in. A few months later, the new guy was spending the night at my house. We were fast asleep when I was woken up by my doorbell ringing over and over. I got up and went downstairs, wondering who could be at my door after midnight. It was Lawrence.

"Why are you here?"

"My car broke down, can I come in?"

"No"

"Why not?"

"Because I have company."

"Oh a friend?"

"No, the guy I told you about is here."

He gave me the strangest look "Ok, can you drive me to my car, it broke down and I walked over here."

I agreed because I wanted him away from my house. So, I went upstairs, gently woke him up and made an excuse to leave. I said a friend needed a ride. He offered to go with me, but I told him to just stay and rest. I ran back down the stairs in a rush to drop Lawrence off. The ride to his car was quiet. I kept fixing the mirror and toying with my keys. After taking him to his car I returned home. I was shaken by his unexpected pop-up. I sat in front of my house and smoked a blunt to calm down. I looked up and saw him slowly drive by, staring at my house. I was irritated but not surprised. I knew his car wasn't messed up. I took it as him just being nosy and tried to brush it off. However, we weren't together anymore and that type of behavior simply couldn't continue. It was something I planned to address and confronted him about it a few days later. I was not prepared for what I learned. The truth shook me to my core. He told me he broke in through my daughter's window (again). He then walked down the hall, into my bedroom and saw us in the bed. I didn't believe him at first. Even he wouldn't do something like that, I thought. But he told me where my purse and shoes were. Then described my friend's shirt and pants, as well as exactly where they were hanging up. He was angry as he stood over us. But after a few minutes he walked downstairs, let himself out through the front door and then rang the doorbell. I was shaking as he recounted this story. I became genuinely scared for my life. We were completely vulnerable and if he wanted to, he could have killed us both. After so many experiences like this, I finally decided I had enough. I toyed with the idea of a restraining order but was scared to make him angry. A client of mine was a sergeant with the Oakland police department. I told her what was going on, off record, in case something happened to me. I simply didn't know what he was capable of. I trusted God but faith without works is dead. I decided to move. I did not want him knowing where I lived anymore.

Within a few weeks I secured a new place. A cute in-law suite on the back of a large property. It was half the size of my townhouse, but I was ok with that. I was careful and secretive, not mentioning the move to anyone who knew Lawrence. I told the new landlord I worked long hours and would have to move in at almost midnight. I hoped moving that late, in the dark, would prevent him from seeing me. I packed the house and Ricky came over to help with the move. As we loaded the moving van, I looked around constantly. There were butterflies in my stomach as I scanned the street and stared at every parked car. I saw no signs of him. I got a large truck so we could do the move in one trip, lessening the chance of being seen. Hours later I was in my new place and able to breathe a sigh of relief (both literally and figuratively). It was short-lived because the next day Lawrence called. "I see you had your ex-husband help you move."

It continued at the new house. I was scared to date. When I did, I certainly wouldn't bring them to my home. I was also honest with anyone I dealt with, they had to know the situation I was in. I had tried unsuccessfully to get away and any new person deserved to know what was going on. It wouldn't be fair to bring someone unknowingly into that level of craziness. The sad part is Lawrence was dating tons of women. I heard stories all the time. But somehow he still had time to stalk me. Countless evenings I came home from the club, only to see his car parked up the street. Several nights I screamed as a figure darted past my window. Months after we broke up he still had the power. Fear is a bad space to be in. It's unhealthy. I was angry and terrified because he wasn't going to stop. A few months after I moved, my cousin Monica showed up to my house unannounced. She knew she was welcome to come by anytime and didn't need to call. She left the club around 2 AM and didn't want to go all the way home. Apparently, she was knocking and knocking on the door, but I was asleep and not answering. She was out there for about 10 minutes when she heard a noise behind her. She turned around, trying to figure out where the noise was coming from. It was dark and difficult to see. She squinted, looking towards the storage shed in my backyard. There was a man, crouching on top of the structure. With me not answering, she knew she needed to hurry and leave. She had no idea who that was, but it wasn't good. Moving quickly, she got a few blocks away. A car pulled up on her slowly. I was living in east Oakland at the time, there are hundreds of murders a year. She began to think someone was following her and stopped, looking dead in the car. It was Lawrence. I couldn't believe it when she told me. On top of the damn shed? How did you get up there? What were you doing? What the fuck? WE AREN'T TOGETHER!! When I confronted him, his response was "How did she know it was me?". When I pressed him for an explanation he explained. The windows in my bedroom were covered with drapes except for two oddly placed, small windows that sat about a foot from the ceiling. When he climbed on the shed, he could see in my bedroom.

These are just a few examples of what went on. It was toxic. He was obsessive and I was high. Sex and power also played a large part. The sex was amazing, which made it hard to walk away. He admitted he enjoyed the drama, because he loved the make up sex. What he wouldn't admit, was the enjoyment he derived from the fear and control he had over me. What I wouldn't admit, was that being on ecstasy and weed played a huge part in the situation. I knew my dependence on drugs was part of why I had engaged in and allowed this type of behavior for so long. It wasn't all him. I should have cut it off at the first sign of crazy. I shouldn't have been on that insane merry go round with him. It takes two to fight, argue and carry on. I played a part and needed to take responsibility for it. But once I was done, I was done. For so long, I prayed for him to find someone else. Not that I wanted someone else to go through that. More so I was desperate to get away from it myself. I was genuinely worried that he might kill me one day. I blocked his number and moved again a year later. This time he didn't know where I lived. Space from him, allowed me to focus on me. I knew I needed to get clean. So, one day I went cold turkey and stopped taking ecstasy. I still smoked weed and drank occasionally. But I knew this time for real, I was ready to let the hard stuff go. As I honored myself by no longer putting hard drugs in my system, I also honored myself by letting go of a toxic relationship. I learned I would rather be alone than in some mess. There is something so beautiful about being sober. Life should be experienced as it actually is, not through an altered reality. I had been high for so long that being sober was a new experience. Things looked and felt different. Change your mind, change your life. Mindset determines reality. As my mind cleared so did my life. I tried to focus on health and wellness. Except for the occasional phone calls, Lawrence faded away. He knew we weren't healthy together. We both have good and bad aspects to ourselves, like any human. But us together was a dangerous mix. I think in the long run we were both happy to close that chapter. We were both better than who we became in that relationship.

In difficult relationships, it's easy to see what the other person did wrong. But the blinders are often up when it comes to looking at ourselves. It is so much easier to point out other people's faults than to see our own. Yet growth comes from self-examination. We only learn when we are honest with ourselves. After a relationship ends it is so important to do some self exploration. What did you do right and more importantly what did you do wrong? How can you be better? What are your triggers? What are your needs? How can you continue to evolve to the best you possible? I learned that when I fall in love, I tend to ignore reality. I choose to see whatever fits the story I want to believe. I recognized that no conscious decisions can be made from a high polluted mind. I could see the contradiction in the way I was living. I was a loving, present, active parent. I had her every day except the weekends. I went to work and was successfully building a clientele and thriving career. I was responsible financially, had no debt and never paid my rent late. I even graduated with my AA in Social Science while Lawrence and I were together. At the same time I was delusional. I thought all that I was doing, made up for the fact that I was a functioning addict. I lived in a state of constant dissatisfaction. I always wanted more. More drugs to get high. More weed to get numb and forget. It was all a distraction. One day you're going to have to sit with yourself, and hopefully you like the person there.

Thank God I had stopped the ecstasy. But I knew that I needed to be completely sober to create the healthy loving environment I envisioned for me and my child. It's like stepping out of a fog. I knew I wasn't where I wanted to be, but I thanked God for the growth and awareness that was taking place. There were no regrets, only wisdom gained and lessons learned.

It was the end of an era. Closing of a chapter. It's like the picture of success. People think it's a straight line. Actually there are ups and downs, good times and agonizing ones. There's no true success without failures on the way. My next season would be great, but damn it the hard times weren't done yet. I had a few more hurdles coming directly up.

If you want to fly, give up everything that
weighs you down.

-Unknown

Chapter 7- Shear Passion

This next period in my life was birthed from pain. The wins were direct results of the losses. My divorce was final, my relationship with Lawrence was over and it was time to move on career wise. I had gone from homeless just a few years earlier, to making around $80,000 annually. I had grown a large clientele by focusing on professionalism, customer service, quality and deep connections. I had clients calling me when they were going through personal issues. I can't tell you all that I heard standing behind the chair. Clients confided their deepest secrets, which I was honored to hold space for. I was building more than a network; I was developing lifelong relationships. I loved the salon I was at, but began to feel it was time to move on. Because the salon I was at operated on commission only, I took home about 60% of what I earned. I still remember the first day I made $1000. I was so excited despite only taking home about $600. I was grateful, but I felt a nudge inside me. That feeling when you know it is time to go to the next level. I wanted to keep more of my money. On top of that, the energy and vibe were changing. It wasn't bad, I just no longer felt like I fit. I was ready to step out on faith and take charge of my career. There was a certain level of security being at that salon. They provided most of the clients for you. But at this point, I had put in work and had my own clientele. There was absolutely no guarantee they would follow me to a new location, but I was ready to see. I ran into a friend who had opened her own salon. A week later I left to work at her shop. I was grateful to finally be in a booth rental location. That means you pay a set rate per week. You are essentially renting your station, similar to renting an apartment. You owe money whether you work or not. But at least there is a cap on how much you pay. I paid less than $200 a week and saw more money than I ever had in my life. I paid off my booth rental with a fraction of one day's work, then kept the profit from everything else. It was a wonderful feeling, and I couldn't believe how my life had changed. Things were looking up. I liked my new location. Plus, working in a salon is always entertaining. Once my coworker Calvin had this interesting client. You could tell she was agitated from the time she walked in. She kept tapping her foot and fidgeting with her bag. She stood, then sat down, stood then sat down again. "Excuse me! Do you have some scissors?" I looked around realizing she was speaking to me. Against my better judgment I handed them over. She stood in front of the mirror, grabbed a chunk of her weave and began hacking it out of her head. My client gave a small gasp. After a few moments she got most of it out. There were clumps of hair on the floor. Her own hair was wild and all over the place. She smiled in the mirror with a lopsided grin, before sitting back down. I went back to talking with my client, while occasionally glancing over at her. Suddenly she leapt out of her chair, ran to the other side of the salon and began punching a bag. I chewed on my lip, unsure of what to do. My client hopped up and yelled "Ay that's mine!". "Oh sorry girl" she responded before sitting back down. I scanned the room and everyone's eyes were wide. Eventually Calvin finished her hair. It was a beautiful weave with bouncy curls. I breathed a sigh of relief, grateful she was close to leaving. She smiled and looked at him.

"Thank you. I have to go get my money and I'll be back."

"What? You don't have my money?"

Her voice raised a few octaves. "I said I'll be back."

Calvin took a salon towel, twisted it up into a rope and leaned back. "Sis, I am going to drag you over the back of this chair if you don't pay me my money. I promise you won't walk out of here, so you better think about the decision you bout to make."

I shifted my weight before taking a few steps back. I did not want to be in the middle of this. Her eyes looked to the right and then the left of the room. Another client chimed in "Girl please pay him his money". After a few moments, she slowly reached inside of her bra and pulled out the cash. Calvin took it, and as if nothing happened said "Thank you love, it was nice to meet you." I let out a huge breath and a shaky laugh. You never know who will walk in the door and must be prepared to deal with a wide range of people.

After a year at the second salon, it was time to create my own space. I loved the owner but was having issues with another stylist. Out of 5 stylists, there was just one that made life uncomfortable. When this individual walked in the whole vibe changed. And at some point, I was done. I needed to be in control of my environment. I wanted to work with people with whom I vibed. I wanted a space that would be my sanctuary. I was a workaholic. Working 12-15 hour days were regular for me. I needed to enjoy being at work. I also needed my daughter to be with me every single day without, feeling like she was in the way. At times God will make us uncomfortable. In those moments, we can play victim or we can grow. We can fall into negativity, or we can make the conscious choice to be positive even when it's hard. We don't make changes when things are ok. Why would we? Average is comfortable. Even if things aren't great, even if we know they could be better, it is very easy to get used to average. But when things get agonizing, we are forced to change. When a situation is excruciating or extremely uncomfortable, we take action. One stylist was making every day uncomfortable, but I was grateful. Because pain is the catalyst for change. Then through the change, there is growth. Growth which moves us to the next level. The only way to control my environment was to open my own salon. It was time to move on. I looked into a few spaces that I liked, but it didn't pan out for various reasons. One day I noticed a For Rent sign on the way to Mayas school. It was a small complex I had passed hundreds of times without noticing. About 8 units, 2 floors and a small parking lot. It was perfect. I was excited as I called the number on the sign. I had already checked out the building and my heart was set on the largest unit. Huge windows, nice space and perfect for a salon. When I called, I was told I couldn't put a hair salon upstairs. It didn't make sense. But I asked to see one of the downstairs units instead, feeling as if this was where I was supposed to go. We set an appointment and he never showed up. I sat in front for over 30 minutes, calling his phone repeatedly. Frustrated, I decided to leave it alone. My search continued. I spent hours driving looking for units for rent. Every off day I searched for the perfect location. Spaces were hard to find, reasonably priced ones were almost impossible. Everything I came across was $2500 and up for around 600 square feet. A few weeks went by and that particular space kept crossing my mind. I called again and this time I got the owner. Turns out the man who stood me up was his son. He clearly wasn't that interested in running the business. The owner on the other hand was amazing. He met me the next day. He was prompt, communicative and friendly. He assured me he had no problem with a salon upstairs and after a few negotiations, we signed the lease. I was terrified but in a good way. If your dreams don't scare you, they aren't big enough. I was scared to fail but excited at the chance to fly. The day after I signed the lease, I sat in awe. I sank to the floor with tears in my eyes thanking God. It was all mine. I went from sleeping on buses to having a car, apartment and now business.

The space I rented needed a lot of work. Plumbing, electrical, divider walls built, etc. I barely had enough money for all the upgrades. I had been saving, but it was expensive. The equipment alone would cost an additional $10-$15k. I simply couldn't afford the contractor plus the added cost of supplies and equipment. I was determined not to open any credit cards or take out any loans. I would only get what I could afford. The rest could come in time. I wasn't concerned because I knew God would cover me. And still he showed up in ways I didn't expect. A friend was working at a storage facility. She told me a lady was getting ready to lose her unit full of salon supplies. She connected us and I purchased almost everything I needed to start the salon. I got 2 shampoo bowls, 2 shampoo chairs, 4 styling chairs, 4 stations, 4 mirrors, 4 waiting room chairs and even some art. I spent $1500. It was a blessing beyond measure. The equipment I got was valued at over $10,000. It just never ceases to amaze me the way God and the universe shows up to support us.

Getting such an amazing deal on all the equipment made purchasing the small things a breeze. I enjoyed shopping for art, replacing the mirrors and picking out small decorations. For a while the financial strain was gone. That is, until a few months into working with my contractor. I didn't know much about business. But I tried to do everything right. I hired a licensed contractor and had him sign a contract. We talked about my design plans and expectations up front. I thought I was being extra careful. In the beginning the contractor got most of the stuff done correctly. He built a wall in the salon to create a separate area for the shampoo bowls. He installed plumbing and did some electrical work for me. The building was old and needed some work to be able to run the amount of electricity a hair salon needs. Even after he finished something wasn't quite right because if I ran more than 2 dryers at a time, they would all cut off. I couldn't focus on that because I began having another major issue. I was running out of hot water. I was a very busy stylist averaging 8 clients per day. On the weekends, I saw 10-14 clients daily (with the help of an assistant). I needed lots of hot water. I would shampoo 2-3 clients, and then the water would run cold for the next hour. It was so bad I turned the water to cold while rinsing the ends of the hair and only used warm on the scalp. I tried to shampoo the hair as quickly as possible, not able to give each client the time and attention I wanted. In my most desperate moments, I heated up water in a little plug up tea kettle. It was unprofessional and embarrassing. I kept calling the contractor, who claimed he had no idea what was going wrong. He would disappear for weeks without answering. He hadn't finished the work despite being fully paid. To get him to answer, I had to call with my number blocked. And I couldn't afford to just hire someone else. I had put my money into him. At some point, I tricked him into answering. After a bunch of excuses, he agreed to send out Jose, the man who he hired to install the water heater. When Jose arrived, I was informed that I did not have a large enough water heater. The contractor purchased it so I didn't understand how that happened. Jose said he told the contractor from the beginning that size wouldn't work. When I asked why it was still installed, his answer infuriated me. Once you take a water heater out of Home Depot it can't be returned. My contractor bought the wrong size and didn't want to eat the cost of his mistake. Then for months he avoided my calls and claimed to have no idea why I was experiencing issues. After I paid him over six thousand dollars, he wouldn't eat an $800 cost. Or at the very least, be honest with me so I could replace it. Regardless of who was at fault, I needed a

156

water heater that worked. I would have replaced it immediately, had I known. That information was helpful. Not only did I have the source of the problem, but I also knew it was time to cut ties with the contractor. I bought a new water heater then contacted a friend to install it. He only charged me a couple of hundred dollars. The new one worked perfectly, for about a week. Then mid shampoo, the water ran cold again. Despite my immense frustration, everything happens at the right time in the right way. It went cold while I was shampooing my grandmother. I was overwhelmed and began to cry. She witnessed how upset I was, stated she was proud of all I had done without asking for any help and immediately offered to have it done correctly. A week later, Sears came out to fix it. From there on, it worked perfectly. The original contractor never finished his job. Despite our contract and the fact that I could have sued him, I let it go. It wasn't worth it. Life would work it all out. I learned a few lessons there. Don't ever pay in full until a job is complete. Do whatever work I can, by myself. And the importance of finding a good contractor I could trust. Going forward, I did the non-skilled labor and left the rest up to the professionals. I painted, put together furniture and stained the shelves. A few years after I opened, I even laid new floors with my best friend Britney. We placed them down tile by tile. She called me one morning. I told her I was putting in the floors. Without me asking, she showed up to my salon in sweats and spent the entire day helping me out. We have been friends since we were 10 and we have each other's back through everything. This is the type of person she is. Absolutely gorgeous inside and out. Her help that day was needed and appreciated. As my best friend she knew

I wouldn't ask. My salon slowly came together, exactly how I envisioned it. Through it all I had friends to support me. And I grew as both a business owner and an individual. There were moments when I was drained financially, but in so many other ways, I was full. Full with love from my close family and friends. Full of the dreams and vision God gave me. Full of the promises I made to myself and more importantly, the ones I made to my daughter. I was full of excitement for what was to come.

Regardless of the occasional struggles, the salon was going well. In fact, thanks to the struggles I appreciated all that I had. To top it off, I was having fun. My clients are like family. It's so much deeper than hair. Being an intuitive empath deepened my relationships everywhere, especially in the salon. At times I would sense things. I would ask a question that would open a floodgate of emotions. A client would walk in and often I would sense immediately if something was wrong. Brand new clients shared everything from being molested as a child to marriage concerns. Three times I had clients call me late at night, on the verge of committing suicide. I have had clients open up in the chair about the most personal and painful things. Then there were the joyful moments. Doing ladies for their graduations, baby showers and weddings. Getting great news about admissions to schools, phenomenal job offers and new loves. Salons are an oasis. A space to open up about any and everything. Somewhere to come with no judgement. Once I got fully comfortable with the space, I was ready to bring in other stylists. Pretty soon, I had a few ladies renting chairs from me. Mary, my braider, became a lifelong friend. We even got the old crew together, several ladies from the first salon I worked at. Aisha, Nake, Jessie and Sunshine joined me, and it immediately felt like home. It was a fun atmosphere. We would laugh, joke, listen to music, watch TV, talk about men, do a lot of hair and make great money.

One evening, less than a year after I opened my salon, I went out to a nightclub in the city. I headed to San Francisco with Britney, a woman I was dating and a few other friends. We were dressed up, excited and ready for the night. We pulled into the parking lot ready to pregame. I pulled out a bottle of tequila and we all started taking shots. It was cheaper to head inside already a little tipsy, plus that set the mood to party. By the time we walked inside it was close to 11 and the party was in full swing. Lots of drinks, music blasting and tons of people on the dance floor. We grabbed an empty table to drop off our stuff and headed to dance. About an hour later I was ready for another drink, so I grabbed my girlfriend Neesh and headed to the bar. We were hugging, kissing and dancing while we waited for the bartender. She was sweet, beautiful and all my attention was on her. So much so that I didn't notice an issue starting to form on the dance floor. I was snapped into reality when I heard shouting. I turned to see the crowd parting quickly. Fights often signaled the end of a night out in the Bay, so people were quick to react. There were two groups of men facing off in the middle. One group looked like an extra large boy band and were clearly there for some sort of event. There were 15-20 of them dressed in all white. The other group was around 20 men as well. They appeared to be a random group of friends, indicated by the lack of matching attire. Both sides were screaming at each other over the music. This is where the DJ comes in. Songs set the mood and this would have been the perfect time for some Sade or Stevie Wonder. Instead, the DJ decides to play Fuck Them Other Ni**as by C Murder. That song has been starting fights for years. When the beat comes on you can't help but feel aggressive. The lyrics filled the club.

Fuck them other nig**s cause I'm down for my nig**s

Fuck them other nig**s cause I'm down for my nig**s

Fuck them other nig**s, cause I ride for my nig**s

I die for my nig**s, fuck them other nig**s

Thanks DJ. Way to read a room. Within seconds a fight breaks out and I'm stuck on one side with Neesh, separated from Britney and the rest of our friends. Within a few minutes the sea of fighting men breaks apart as someone yells "Gun! He has a gun!" Screaming instantly breaks out from every direction. As both groups of men pull back they are disheveled, facing each other in an old Western style standoff. Some of the men have guns. The ones who don't look frantic. Eyes darting around, probably looking for a weapon or an escape. A handful of men ran into the kitchen area of the club. They burst back through the doors with huge butcher knives. Words were being exchanged that I couldn't make out. A few moments later "Pop! Pop!" Everyone starts running. There's screaming and panic everywhere. I see blood and broken glass on the ground. I don't know if people cut themselves or if someone has been shot. It was too much going on to find Britney. I grabbed Neesh's hand and ran. I pulled her behind the bar thinking we could hide there. At least 40 other people had the same idea and were already in that spot. My eyes were drawn immediately to a man in all white. Knowing he was a part of all this, I didn't want to hide anywhere near him. The last thing I needed was to be next to him and have someone shoot in our direction. Still clutching Neesh's hand I spun around and took off running. Off to the side I noticed a tiny spot. With my heart racing and palms sweating I yanked her to the ground, pulling us both against the wall. My legs felt like jelly as I looked around, trying to figure out what to do. I was finally still long enough to check my phone. Some people were still crouching down hiding, others were pushing their way outside the cub. I looked down as Britney was calling my phone.

"Where are you?"

She replied in a whisper "I'm right outside the club, hiding behind the door. Hella people are running by me."

She was shielded between the door and the wall. I wanted us all to be together. I wanted to run outside to her. But something told me clearly Don't go out those doors. I looked up and saw another friend we came with, walking slowly towards the exit. I left Neesh and ran to the girl. She looked dazed and confused as I snatched her hand and pulled her back. I was shaking as I jerked her to the ground. "Why aren't we leaving! They stopped shooting in here. We gotta get out of here now. We can't be in here. They have guns!" She was desperate to get

161

outside. I was just as desperate to stay in that exact spot. I clearly heard a voice (albeit in my head) tell me not to move. I wasn't budging. A few moments later they started shooting right outside the door. "Run!" I screamed at Britney through the phone. The security guard yanked the door closed and locked it to keep the shooters out. That completely exposed Britney and she literally ran for her life. I don't know if I've ever been more scared. There were still men with guns and knives inside and now outside was just as wild. I prayed and begged God. "Please, I have a daughter. She needs me. I'm begging you. I have to get home to my child. She can't be raised without a mother. I'm begging you. Please, please, please! I'm so scared." With my plea out the way I focused back on Britney. I could hear gunshots through the phone. She told me they were shooting back and forth across the street. One of the shooters was standing a few feet from her. A woman grabbed her screaming "Are we going to die?!" I told her to get on the ground and get under the car. I was so scared for all of us. I hated that my best friend in the whole world was outside alone.

It felt like forever, crouched in our hiding spot. I alternated between prayers and looking around to see what was going on. I was flooded with relief when we heard a loud bam bam bam on the door. "Open up! It's SFPD!" Everyone got up and cautiously came out of the club, one by one and grateful to be alive. There were police officers in every direction, ready with guns drawn. Sure no one would try anything now, I finally felt safe. I went straight to Britney, grabbing her and finally able to smile. We continuously thanked God we were all ok. I was still shaking from the adrenaline as we walked to my car. I took a few deep breaths to relax the knots in my stomach, focusing on placing one foot in front of the other because my legs still felt weak. As we got closer, we were met with caution tape and paramedics. My car was considered a part of a crime scene because one of the men was shot a few feet away. Had we left the club the first time we would have been in the line of fire. We spent the evening outside in the cold waiting for my car to be released. We were emotionally exhausted, tired and hungry. But I had to go to work at 7 in the morning and was hoping to leave with my car. Regardless we were alive and grateful. We literally laughed and joked the entire time, making the most of the situation. We huddled up to stay warm, danced and took pictures until my phone died. At 6 am public transportation started running again and we were able to leave. I made it to work right on time. My car wasn't released for several days because it was considered a part of evidence. I didn't go out for a long time after that. I took that as a sign to change the type of events I went to. Clubs no longer felt safe.

One day I received a call that would change my life. A friendly voice on the other end had some great information. Rebecca shared the vision and purpose of her non-profit, Haircuts with Heart. She was looking for local stylists to come out to events she was organizing. She needed volunteers to do free haircuts and styles for homeless and underserved members of society. I was 100% in from day one. I always wanted to give back. I went to homeless encampments to drop off clothes and pans of food. I donated money to some homeless people I passed on the street. And I took used items to the Goodwill. I had done a few things here and there, but the thought of putting together a whole event was overwhelming. Britney was working at a homeless shelter around that time. She handpicked and sent women to the salon. I performed their services for free. I had 2 days a month where I took clients from the shelter. It felt good but limited. Working with Rebecca would allow me to have a bigger impact. She was organized, connected and ready to go. Her operation allowed us to service people on a more frequent basis. Our first event was in downtown Oakland. We did hair for young ladies who were victims of sex trafficking and sexual exploitation. Some of these girls were as young as 13. I focused on the joy we created instead of the sadness of their stories. Their faces lit up when they saw their reflections in the mirror. Their happiness was so rewarding. From there, I did dozens of events with Rebecca. Sometimes we went to East Oakland, setting up tables, chairs and mirrors outside on the street. We created a mini salon near homeless encampments, using generators for power. We stayed for hours, servicing long lines of homeless men and women. Some events we partnered with other organizations like Lava Mae, who provide mobile showers and laundry. Every month we went to Roots Community Center where some of the clients became friends. Other times we went to Kaiser and volunteered at their annual prom. It was painful but rewarding. We dolled up children with cancer and terminal illnesses, taking their minds off reality. There was one little girl in particular who kept my attention. She walked into the hair and makeup room slowly, as if every step hurt. She had on a beautiful pink dress covered in sparkles, with a white sash around her belly. The dress hung loosely on her shoulders, with her thin frame peeking through. Her hair was mostly gone, with approximately two inches of brown hair spread out unevenly across her head. She went to the first empty chair, sighing as she sat down. She was silent, shoulders slumped and kept rubbing her beautiful blue eyes. My lip trembled as I held back tears, trying to refocus on the child in my chair. A nurse walked up and rubbed her shoulder, before leaning in and whispering "Sweetie I'm so glad you decided to come." The little girl looked up and smiled. It was a reminder of why we were there. We couldn't change their circumstances, but we could shift their focus for one day. Despite the sadness of seeing sick children, we were grateful to bring them a little joy. Together we were at a variety of events around the Bay Area, servicing as many people as we could. We volunteered with veterans, at kids clubs, homeless shelters for teens and anywhere where there were people who wanted a haircut. When I started volunteering I had never done a men's cut. But that was the need. Even for homeless women, long hair didn't make sense. So, I learned on the spot and got better every time. It started rough, but pretty soon, I could do a decent taper. It fed my soul. It meant so much to give back regularly. The stories I heard, the people I connected with. The most important part of what we do, is making individuals feel seen. You can't know how powerful that is to a person who is used to being ignored. When your very presence is an irritation, when your existence is a bother, the world doesn't feel like a kind place. It filled us all with so much joy to go in and pamper people. I thanked God for letting me be of service. I cut a man's hair the same day he got out of the hospital. With the wristband still on his arm, he shared the terminal prognosis he received the day before. He had brain

165

cancer. I shaved his hair with tears in my eyes. I spoke to a woman who didn't recognize her own son on the street. She was addicted to crack for so many years she had lost everything. Her home, job, health, awareness, children and self respect were gone. I could feel her shame as she recounted the story. Another woman confided she had 5 children, all of whom were taken by CPS. One found her on Facebook and wanted to meet her. He sent her a ticket, hoping she would come visit. She never showed up. She admitted she couldn't leave the drugs behind long enough to go. I learned early to never ask about children, it was too touchy. Instead of asking questions I tried to provide the space for people to talk about whatever was on their mind. Often, people opened up without prompt. Because I had been homeless and struggled with addiction, I understood. Sometimes you look up and don't recognize who you've become. There was no judgment on my end and I think they felt that. If anything, I thanked God over and over that my story was different. It was a constant reminder of how far I had come. I was so grateful to be in a position to help and brighten someone's day. I loved all the events but the most rewarding ones were the ones with children. They have always been my soft spot. These events were so healing to me, maybe more so than for the people we serviced. So, no matter what was going on in my personal life, I showed up. Once, we did an event that partnered with Steph Curry. We set up with other non-profits who offered everything from a meditation bus to groceries. We cut until it got dark, finishing the last men using the light from the streetlamps. My daughter was with me. She spent the whole day assisting us and several other groups. The coordinator of the event was so impressed with her she made sure she left with a signed basketball. Steph and Ayesha Curry were kind enough to take a selfie with my baby. I hope she's learning lessons with these events. The perks were nice. But I brought her to learn about life, gratitude and service.

After years of being disappointed and angry with myself, I was proud and it was a welcome change. I knew I was giving life my all. I showed up consistently trying to be the best me possible. Despite my mistakes (and I made lots of them) I could look at myself in the mirror knowing I was trying my best. It was paying off because, overall, life was going well. I was making over $100,000 a year. I had my work published in a black bridal magazine Munaluchi Bridal. I was happy and comfortable with who I was. Spiritually I was digging deeper. I still went to church, but I also read books on different world religions. I studied some of the Koran and a lot of Kabbalah. I meditated and did yoga. I wanted to be more connected to the universe and myself. My life had completely changed, and I was so grateful. I learned how to better handle difficult situations. Like when a person I considered a friend, stole my credit cards and drained my account. I was hurt and I cried. Then I was ok. I got the money back from the bank. I actually felt sorry for the person who did it, because I knew it came from a place of desperation. I also honored myself enough to permanently walk away from this person, with no hard feelings. I was frequently asked how I dealt so well with trauma. I explained I felt the same emotions but learned to shift my perspective, elevate my maturity and handle it with a little more grace.

I was working 7 days a week and only took off for Kamaya. She was raised in the salon. I had a desk in the corner where she did her homework. She spent hours playing, reading and hanging out with me. She has always been my little best friend. And I always tried to be the best mother I could. I'm sure there will be things she wishes I did differently. It is the nature of children to focus on what they are missing. But I am comfortable in how I raised her. Within a few years of the divorce I had her 95% of the time. The absence from her dad caused her depression and anxiety. I spent many nights comforting her and wiping her tears. Unsure of the best way to handle it, I put her in counseling. Over time she got better. The further her dad faded from her life, the closer her and I became. My mother and Kenny also played a huge part in her life. My mom made up for the past by being the most loving, present and attentive grandmother my child could ask for. She was willing to keep her any time. I am not the mother that sends my kids to their grandmothers every week, or even every month. But it was nice to know the option was there. She was never allowed to spend the night with friends. I did my best to protect her. Outside of our time together, I made sure to focus on her education and be her advocate in every way possible. I had to approach teachers and administrators who were not treating her appropriately. Quite often, I feel, because of the color of her skin. When I felt like she was in a racist environment at her elementary school, I took her out. She moved to a charter school that focused on teaching and uplifting black and brown children. I spent thousands putting her in sylvan tutoring to make sure she was on target academically. I kept her in competitive cheer and was the team mom. I purchased a heat press and together we customized everything from shirts to make up bags for the girls. Although many people called me a workaholic, my clients knew my daughter came first. And eventually I was ready to expand my family. I wanted to settle down. As with anything else in life, that would come with its own set of challenges.

Accept what is, let go of what was, and have faith in what will be

-Unknown

Chapter 8- Agape

I was tired of pain and heartache, wondering if I would ever find the one. I consistently came across two situations. I would catch feelings for "the project." An amazing individual with a lot of potential, but not ready for a relationship. The person consistently between jobs, houses and goals. Situations are temporary, so material things don't matter to me. Yet, I wanted someone with major goals and ambitions. A person who envisioned the same type of future I was looking to create. I had to learn to stop feeling guilty for no longer wanting to struggle. It had been almost a decade since I was sleeping on buses but I felt guilty for having high expectations. I wanted a spouse who could also help me when times get rough. In my experience "the projects" were ready to settle down immediately. They wanted to be at my door, bag in hand on day one. I felt like it was a matter of convenience. They wanted the lifestyle I was becoming accustomed to without the work attached. I simply wasn't willing to work 12 hours a day and come home to someone lying on my couch. I wasn't interested in paying for everything every time we went out, but I also didn't want to miss out on experiences because my spouse couldn't afford to go. I did not want to feel like I was buying love. I would rather be single.

The second type I was coming across was the "Mr. or Ms. Unavailable." This individual had it all together. They were established and comfortable in terms of career, home and finances. We vibed. We went out to eat, spoiled each other and even vacationed together. Everything felt right until it was time to settle down. Then I realized they wanted the relationship without the title. Which really meant they weren't interested in commitment, at least not with me. But instead of being honest, they wanted to play house, talk every day, and see each other every week. It was frustrating and confusing. They would express their interest, even a few claimed to love me. Yet, commitment was too much. Lastly there were the situations where the timing wasn't right. I met amazing people but it wasn't meant to be. Like this beautiful woman, who was a teacher and activist. To this day she continues to inspire me. Or this Jamaican man who was smart, funny and loved to cook. We laughed and talked for hours. For whatever reason, it wasn't working. As a result, I learned to recognize and accept reality sooner. I wasn't going to try to force anything. If I didn't see a future I was moving on.

Everything happens for a reason. It sounds so cliche right? Truly believing it will change your life. There are two main approaches to difficult situations. Let's look at the end of a relationship. The first, and most common, is to cry, complain and feel like a victim. To be angry at the person who misled you. To be furious at the broken promises. But what can you gain from that? How will that help you move forward? More importantly how will it help you create a different future? The other approach is to take accountability and grow through the pain. To be honest with yourself about how you can be better. To understand pain and heartbreak is how we grow. I learned from every person I dated. I gained a deeper understanding of who I was and how to be better. I also discovered what I need in a relationship. I was meeting good people, we just weren't meant for each other. After a series of projects, unavailables and not the right times I reconnected with an ex.

He wasn't just any old fling. He was The ex. I felt like I loved him forever. He was my first kiss. Someone I had butterflies for my whole life. He lived about an hour away but the distance didn't bother me. I was so excited when we found each other again. We were back dating and I was all in. For months I would drive back and forth to see him every Saturday night. On the evening of July 3 I was woken up by a phone call. My heart fluttered when I saw his name on the screen. "Hey babe" I mumbled, still half asleep. My smile instantly dropped. The last thing I expected was a woman's voice. We stayed on the phone for 45 minutes. The details of our conversation don't matter. We were cordial but it was painful. By the time we got off it was clear that I was not the only woman he was with. While I didn't believe half of what this stranger was telling me, there was enough truth for me to be heartbroken. It was midnight and she was calling me from my boyfriend's phone. I was so disappointed, again. Tears wet my pillow as I drifted back to sleep.

The sun began to creep in and it felt good on my face. For a moment I forgot the details of the previous night. I lay there for a few moments before it all came back. I quickly rolled over to grab my phone, anxiously checking to see if he called. Nothing. Kamaya was with her dad for the holiday. He was with this woman. I was at home with my cat. I needed time to think. Nature has always been medicinal to me so I decided to go for a hike. I rolled a blunt on the way knowing it would numb my emotions. When I arrived, the fresh air felt wonderful. The hike was therapeutic and the silence was healing. Still, he crossed my mind every few minutes. I walked for about an hour trying to resist checking my phone. I tried to stay present but it was hard to focus. By the time I got back to my car I couldn't help it and anxiously grabbed my phone. I was hoping for a barrage of missed calls and texts. Apologies and explanations. A long message explaining that this was all some big mistake. Something showing he cared. Instead there was nothing. I was trying so hard to be strong but I lost it. I burst into tears again and cried the whole drive home. He was with another woman and it hurt. He was laying in bed with someone else while I was on an emotional roller coaster. I felt stupid. He clearly didn't even care enough to call. I wasn't sure if he knew she reached out to me. Regardless I felt completely unimportant. The biggest sting was that I would have to let him go. No matter what, I knew we were over. My heart wanted to wait for some excuse. My mind knew the excuses didn't matter. When I got home I blocked his number and that chapter was done. I had to close my heart to someone I had loved since I was 14. I knew I needed a different approach to dating. I didn't want to reconnect with any exes. I didn't want to meet anyone at a bar. Insanity is doing the same thing expecting a different result. It was time to try something new. I decided to make a dating account on Match.com. I had never tried online dating before but figured it was worth a shot. This was one of those examples of God closing doors to steer you to the ones meant for you. Had that painful situation not happened, and all the other ones before, I wouldn't have made it to my destiny.

As someone who always met partners the old fashioned way, I was hesitant to try online dating. I grew up during a time where it was something you thought desperate people did. There was definitely a stigma attached. However I saw it work for so many clients in my salon. In one year I saw five women meet and marry men they met online. Hearing their stories and seeing their love develop was beautiful. It inspired me to try it for myself. I took some time to create a profile that was a reflection of what I really wanted. Lots of men reached out to me but in the end I only went on a handful of dates. There were so many handsome, educated men. But there were deal breakers that popped out instantly. Anyone who wasn't interested in marriage or children was a dealbreaker. Spirituality was also a make or break. You have to know what you want in order to get it. You can't just be open to whoever is interested in you. I need to be spiritually aligned with whoever I am with. Of course there is nothing wrong with being atheist. And I completely respect all spiritual beliefs. However, I wanted to share a similar viewpoint with my spouse. I wanted to align on the deepest levels possible, with anyone I would be building a life with. I systematically went through my checklist. Then if I felt we were aligned on the big issues, I was open to dating.

Online dating was an interesting experience. The first few dates were bland. There were no sparks on either side. We ended it politely, both knowing it would be our only meeting. The third man I went out with was a handsome white guy I was super excited to meet. He was about two years older than me. I have always preferred older men, preferably at least 10 years older, so he was on the young side. But I thought we matched up pretty well so I decided to try it out. Britney and I dubbed him "the conductor" due to this cute hat he wore in one of his pictures. We met up in San Francisco and headed out for dinner. I was impressed as we arrived at a cute little place on the water. We sat and talked over a couple glasses of wine. He was nice but not what I expected. The more he talked the quieter I got. My internal dialogue on the other hand was on a roll. "He is really cute. His eyes are pretty, but wow they are big. Why is he moving so much? He seems high. Are your pupils supposed to be big or small? I'm so confused, something seems off about this guy. Is it me? Maybe I shouldn't have smoked before the date." As if on cue, he interrupted my train of thought with an animated exclamation.

"I don't do drugs, I don't know why no one ever believes me". I did my best to maintain a straight face. I mean how do you respond to that statement? Especially when he looks high as a kite. Instead, I changed the subject.

"Sooooo what do you do for a living? My best friend and I call you the conductor because of your hat. Do you work on trains or something?"

He laughed "No, I'm a doorman at a hotel."

"Oh" I gave a small smile.

"Yeah when I was younger I didn't care about school or a career. I kinda just went with the flow. That didn't work out that well for me. Who knew women actually like men with goals and ambition?"

I couldn't hold back my laughter any longer. "Yeah who would have thought"

There was no chance of us going out again, but he was definitely entertaining. I laughed through most of dinner, even when I didn't think he was joking. When we finished we headed to my car. The drive to his house was pretty quiet so I turned on the music to fill the space.

"Thanks so much for dropping me off, I'm going to try to get a car soon." I nodded. "Oh and do you need to use the bathroom before you head back over the bridge?". I declined. "Good! I have roommates and try not to bring anyone upstairs". I smiled. "Plus our place is kind of bare. Kinda like Coming to America, except I'm not a prince."

Again, I burst into laughter. This guy was hilarious. Before he got out of the car he gave me a smile, followed by an awkward hug. He called a few days later and asked if I wanted to go out again. I politely declined.

The next date made me want to give up. It was less entertaining and also lacked chemistry. That's the nature of life, we tend to give up right before the breakthrough. Despite the fact that we are usually one failure away from success. You literally can not fail if you keep trying. And you can not succeed if you give up. I'm glad I stuck it out because I met a man I really liked. He was fine as hell. Dominican and Peruvian, a few inches taller than me. He had thick black hair and beautiful hazel eyes. He also spoke Spanish which was a major turn on. I loved the allure of men from another country. On top of that the conversation just flowed. He was chill, relaxed and we enjoyed each other's company. He was intelligent, financially secure and well established. He worked in Tech, owned multiple homes and cars, but was still humble. In fact, I knew nothing about how much he made for months. From the beginning he showed me I could trust him. He left his phone face up on the table when he went to the restroom. He was open, honest and direct. We went from hanging out every other weekend, to seeing each other several times a week. I was in heaven. I literally felt like I met my knight in shining armor. He was everything I was looking for. Smart, successful, kind, easy going and handsome. I had to pinch myself to know it was real. One weekend he asked me to come to his house before our date. When I pulled up he asked me to come inside. Standing in the living room was his sister, brother and daughter. My eyes widened as I glanced from person to person, I wasn't expecting to meet his family. Then with a wide smile, I embraced everyone in a hug. At that moment I realized how serious he was.

Before Esteban I had a six month rule. I didn't want another boyfriend, I was ready for a husband. I refused to commit to anyone before six months because I wanted us to truly get to know each other before jumping into a relationship. With him it was different. It was a whirlwind romance. Pretty quickly we were shutting down our Match profiles and in three months we made it official. We were so excited to have found each other. It was like a breath of fresh air in a stuffy room. Light at the end of a tunnel you thought you'd be trapped in forever. We were constantly trying to outdo one another. For our first Valentine's day together I surprised him with a cruise to Mexico. It would be the first vacation for all four of us (we were bringing Kamaya and his daughter Jasmine). His gift for me was a surprise trip to the San Diego safari park. We spent three days zip lining, taking a safari and going out to romantic dinners. I was finally happy, floating on cloud nine. We loved spending time together and our kids clicked immediately. At the time Kamaya was 6 and Jasmine was 7. They were oddly similar. Kamaya liked to dance and Jasmine liked to sing. They never got tired of talking, laughing and playing together. They had so much fun from the very start. They were even the exact same size. Short, slim and tiny for their age. It was kismet.

Our family cruise was so much fun that a few months later we went back alone. An adults only vacation was in order. At one of the destinations we decided to leave the boat for some excursions. We figured a moped would be a fun way to get around. I was nervous because I can be pretty clumsy but felt comfortable with the decision that Esteban would drive. He went to grab the moped while I waited in front. My nerves grew when I saw him wobbling down the street. I did the only logical thing. I took a shot of tequila and hopped on the back. What could go wrong? The take off was shaky but the ride smoothed out pretty quickly. We cruised to the beach and I started to get more comfortable. We planned on smoking some weed and relaxing by the water. We lit the blunt as we walked through the sand, assuming the fresh air would blow away the strong scent of Cali weed. A man walking by called out "You shouldn't do that". We looked at each other, but before we could make a move we saw red and blue lights coming in our direction. Esteban stomped out the weed a few seconds before they reached us but the haze of smoke was still fresh in the air. The officer jumped out of the car screaming and yelling. Before I knew it Esteban was in cuffs and the contents of his pockets were strewn on the hood of the vehicle. Weed, a vape pen and some money were crumpled in a heap. They were speaking so quickly in Spanish I couldn't follow. But I realized quickly the cop wanted money. I pulled everything I had out of my bra and handed it over. The cop smiled. That was the magic answer because immediately after Esteban was released from his cuffs and we were allowed to leave. The cop walked away with almost $300, our weed and vape pen. I was literally shaking as I climbed on the back of the moped. I held tightly to Esteban as we pulled off slowly, with the cop right behind. When we got to the light, he pulled up next to us, handed us the weed and motioned to the right, as if to say go smoke over there. You would think we would have gone straight back into town. The cop might overlook it a second time, but God was trying to tell us something different. Instead, we wanted to get high even more. We drove until we found an empty space behind an abandoned building. We rolled up, smoked and drank the last of the alcohol. Feeling a false sense of empowerment, I got the bright idea to drive us back to town. Esteban nodded in agreeance, seemingly unconcerned. I needed to make a right out of the complex to get back on the street. From there it was a straight shot back to town. Instead of turning the moped in the direction I wanted to go, I figured I would maneuver it like a car. I pressed the gas and we peeled off, startled by how quickly we shot across the street. We went so fast I never turned to align with traffic. Instead, we went 5 feet and crashed into the divider wall. We were in a huge tangled pile on the cement. Esteban was on top of the moped, which in turn was on top of me. As I lay there, I wondered how I ended up on the bottom of the heap. Trying to catch my breath, I slowly pulled myself. Cars were whizzing by in both directions and I thanked God for that divider. It was the only thing stopping us from driving directly across the freeway onramp. I was in so much shock I didn't feel the pain until I got up. I had scratches, bruises and road rash all over my body. Even my toenail was cracked. Everything burned except my face. I reached up quickly, feeling my cheeks, forehead and chin. My face was spared. I smiled at the silver lining and focused on that to stop the tears. The hood had fallen off the moped and it was covered in dents and scratches. Chunks of paint were missing from both sides. Esteban was fine minus one little scratch on his leg. At least one of us was alright. The worst part was that we had to get the moped all the way back to the rental place. I insisted on walking back. Getting back on the moped felt like a death sentence. After hobbling for less than a block in the scorching sun, I realized there was no way I could walk all the way back. I said a prayer as we shoved the hood back in place and I climbed on the back. The first few blocks were uneventful. Then we pulled up to a light. When the moped stopped the hood plunged to the ground. Everyone was staring. I avoided making eye contact as I climbed off the back, retrieved the hood and tucked it under my arm. It stayed there for the entire ride back. I was nervous about what we would be charged but the owner smiled and said it happens all the time. We only owed $150. If I knew crashing was common, we would have taken a taxi around town.

Even the "bad" incidents were good. We had fun. We learned more about each other as we explored life. We became better people, parents and partners. Within a year we were combining families and moving in together. That was a big deal. The last man I lived with was Ricky. Stability was so important. Especially since I had Kamaya. After my past experiences I cherished my living situation. After Ricky and I split I always had a nice home. It was clean, spacious and comfortable. Kamaya always had her own room fully decked out with toys, clothes and lots of pink. Making sure Maya had her own space was a non negotiable. I promised myself she would always feel safe and comfortable at home. I made sure she had her own room from the day she was born. I didn't live in a rich area, but my home was my sanctuary and something I would never take for granted. For me to move in with Esteban was scary but exciting. It took a lot of vulnerability. But it was worth a leap of faith.

One of the benefits of living together was being able to do more things as a family. We enrolled the girls in competitive cheerleading and it became their passion. It is gymnastics based and includes intense flips and tumbling. They made up routines and spent hours flipping around the backyard. They were both flyers (the cheerleader that goes in the air) and even ended up the same team every year. One year they didn't like their place in a portion of the routine. They were essentially just standing there until it was time for them to go into a stunt. They spent a whole afternoon creating their own choreography for that portion. At the next practice they put it into the routine as casually as if it was there from the start. I sat with the other parents watching, amazed no one noticed. Later on when some tweaks were being made to the team's choreography, another girl got added to their spot. They taught her the 16 count as well. It was pretty impressive that they could make up something that fit into a professional routine. And once they started to travel and compete, it became an excuse for a family vacation. We ended up in Florida, Oregon, Washington, Vegas, LA and Dallas. We started a tradition. Whenever we traveled for a competition we visited at least one neighboring state. One year in Dallas, we drove to Louisiana to explore. Another Dallas trip landed us in Oklahoma. After a competition in Vegas, we drove to see the Grand Canyon. We had a blast stopping at small motels on the way, eating local food and staying up late gazing at the stars. We explored most of the United States this way.

The first few years flew by. We really got to know one another and fell deeply in love. We even bought our first house. It was a beautiful 3 bedroom home in the hills. Almost every day there were deer on our front lawn.

We had fun remodeling, decorating and making it a home. Then like any relationship, we started having growing pains. We were very different people. We were blending different backgrounds, cultures and lifestyles. We had some contradictory views on life. The additional stress of combining families began to take a toll. Especially when it came to our parenting styles. I tried to guide and direct the kids' path. I was loving and involved. A team mom, volunteer at the school type parent. But I was also strict. I lived by a phrase my grandma used to say. To whom much is given much is required. Meaning I will give you the world, but I expect you to try your absolute best in every area of your life. I expect good grades. More importantly I require high morals and good character. I constantly reminded the kids that your character is who you are when no one is looking. It is what you would do in a situation where you knew you wouldn't get caught. As a parent it is our duty to raise good human beings who are an asset to this world. While Esteban cares about those things, he has a very different approach. His parenting style is a lot more relaxed. He felt like kids will naturally turn out alright. If you love them, invest in them and cherish them they will be fine. Discipline really isn't a part of his parenting. Over the years that created a lot of tension and arguments between us. It almost drove us apart. But we eventually met in the middle. I learned to relax on a lot of issues. I realized that despite my intentions, at times I was harsh. I began to appreciate the beauty of going with the flow. Not every behavior needed to be corrected. When correction was necessary, I needed a more gentle approach. I came to see the rigidity I had placed on myself was being projected on the kids. And it wasn't fair. We were able to learn from each other when we stopped trying to be right. So often we got closed off, defensive and shut down. From there we missed out on the lessons, growth and blessings. Through uncomfortable critique we both learned to be better parents, both individually and as a unit. Eventually Esteban learned the importance of stepping out of a friend role and giving more direction. I learned to take a softer, more gentle approach. One in which mistakes are celebrated as a good thing because that's how we learn.

What came natural, was our mutual desire to expose our children to different cultures and places. We wanted to show them the world. We weren't the type of parents to travel and leave the kids behind. When we went on trips we took the whole crew. The cheer travel tradition continued on every vacation. We went to New York once, and took a road trip down half the East Coast. We stopped in Philadelphia to visit Noel, then drove to Delaware and Maryland. We left excited to check off four more states. In Cuba we attempted to drive from one side to the other. We piled 7 people in a classic ford model T after finding a man willing to give us a ride. What we didn't expect was for him to bring his wife. Normally I would say the more the merrier, but in this case the back was quite cramped. We couldn't go above 50 mph for fear of the car overheating. And every time it rained we pulled over because the windshield wipers didn't work. Still, it was a wonderful opportunity to practice my Spanish. I insisted on having my own conversations and didn't allow Esteban or my father-in-law translate for me the entire trip. Eventually we settled on the halfway mark, a random town that we picked when we couldn't take another minute in the car. We took excursions in Jamaica, visiting The Duns Waterfall and a local school. We tried coconut water as a family, surprised at the bitter taste. In Atlanta we were exposed to so much history. The plantation tours in Louisiana were a sobering experience. We enjoyed boats down the Bayou and trying alligator for the first time. In D.C. we walked through the Holocaust museum with tears in our eyes, devastated by the horrors that have been committed. We enjoyed the parks in Oregon and Washington, then played on the beaches in Hawaii. The life we created was amazing but not without trials.

Our trip to Hawaii started perfectly. Despite hours of travel time, as soon as we made it to the hotel we were ready to have fun. We threw our luggage to the side and put on our swimsuits. We laughed and giggled the whole way to the hotel pool. Esteban and I lounged on the side while the girls swam. I was happy but tired.

"I don't feel like swimming, I'm going to let you get in with the girls."

"Ok babe, I'm going to relax here for a bit first."

I responded "Actually let me take off my shorts before one of these girls starts drowning and I have to jump in and save them." He smirked as I got undressed.

"We both know I am the better swimmer."

I rolled my eyes "You're definitely not boo. I've been swimming since I was four". We both laughed.

We joked back and forth for a few more minutes before I laid back and pulled out a book. It was a beautiful day. Hot, humid and gorgeous. I was snapped out of my trance when I heard "Mommmmmmyyyyyy Jazz is drowning!" The tone of her voice sent chills down my spine. We know the sound of our children when they are terrified. I jumped up and looked out to the pool. There was a look of terror on Jasmine's face. She was in the deepest area of the pool splashing around frantically. She couldn't scream. Water was in her face and mouth, and her life vest was around her neck. She was panicking. I threw my book to the side and took off in a full sprint to the pool. I dove into the water and swam as fast as I could in her direction. My mind was blank and adrenaline was pumping. When I reached her I used all my energy to scoop her up and lift her above my head. She clutched on to me as I swam us both to the edge of the pool. Her face was red and she had tears in her eyes. I looked over at Esteban, he made it a few steps away from his chair. Thankfully my bonus baby was ok. I checked her over and over again to make sure she was alright, glaring at the adults nearby who didn't attempt to help. We all clambered out of the pool, ready to take a break. Once the fear and panic subsided, I nudged him and said "I told you so". He replied "Damn, that's exactly what you said was going to happen." Our next few vacations were filled with wonderful memories. Scary moments are inevitable. Rough patches are a part of life. But we got through them together as a family. We learned from those moments and were more careful going forward. We took heed to the lessons. We continued to experience different people, religions and ways of life. But safely. We enjoyed instilling a broader world view in our children and ourselves. That is why we traveled. It's in those moments that we thrived.

About 3 years into our relationship, we were arguing a lot. It felt like we were treading water instead of progressing in the relationship. I needed a break and decided to get away with Britney. I wanted enough time away to clear my head. We decided to go to Barcelona, Spain. It turned into the most amazing trip ever. It is still one of my favorite places in the world. We rented a room with a kitchenette where we could cook our daily meals. We went to local grocery stores to buy our food. Most days were spent exploring. The Catalan Gothic architecture was breathtaking. The buildings were unlike anything I'd ever seen. We toured the city by bus, hopping on and off all day. Then spent the evenings on the shore of the Mediterranean Sea. We visited the Museu D' Historia De Barcelona. It housed what was left of an ancient city. We walked underground and got a glimpse of life long ago. It is the largest Roman excavation outside of Rome. The trip was filled with beautiful experiences and an extra surprise came out of that vacation. In Europe it's common to mix weed with tobacco. I have never been a tobacco smoker, probably thanks to my parents. The way they reacted to cigarette smoked rubbed off on me and I never had the desire to try it. I still smoked weed but was not going to sneak it on a plane. So by default I ended up on a 2 week vacation with no weed. I could have asked around for some when we got there. Weed is world wide. But we had so much fun I didn't need it. Plus, Britney has never been a smoker so that made it easier. Before I knew it we had been there a week. That was the longest I had ever gone without weed (except for when I was pregnant). I was proud of myself and determined to continue when I got home, but life has a way of testing us. There are moments when we have to prove that we are who we say we are. Especially after we change. That moment came one morning as I was getting dressed. I reached in a coat pocket and felt something familiar. There was a small blunt. My heart rate increased. I knew I was in a sticky situation. It is a lot harder to resist when the drug is in your hand. I held it for close to 10 minutes. I was trying to fight my temptation to smoke it. In life we are always confronted with the things we want to change. If your issue is cheating you will continually come across someone you find attractive. If alcohol is your temptation, friends will pop up with a bottle of wine. The truth is that these moments give us an opportunity to resist. When we do so successfully we grow stronger. That enforces the change. Of course I didn't think about all that in the moment, I was just trying not to smoke the blunt. Finally I jumped up and threw it into the bathroom wastebasket. Moments later, without a word, Britney walked in the bathroom and I heard a flush. That is why she is my best friend. She has always had my back. She was being stronger for me, than I could be for myself. I would have grabbed the blunt right out the garbage and she knew that. Flushing it down the toilet saved me. I never smoked weed again.

A few months after we returned to the States, I shot straight up in the middle of the night. My heart was beating so hard I felt like it would jump out of my chest. Disoriented, I looked around. With a sigh of relief I realized I was in my bed. Why do I keep having this dream? Over and over, it was the same thing. It's late at night and I'm on a dark street. I think I'm in a van. I get out of the car and walk up to a person or people. I don't see anyone, but I know I'm not alone. Then it switches and I am running. Desperate and scared. Fleeing something. I keep thinking if I can make it to this corner I'll be alright. I was trying so hard. I need to make it to the corner, I need to make it to the corner. All of a sudden I'm not running anymore. There was no pain but I know I was hit. There was a distinct awareness I was shot. As I dropped to the ground all the fear was gone. I knew I was never getting up. A figure wearing a black hoodie stood over me, but the face I couldn't make out. I was calm, it was over.

I had this dream, or some variation of it, for months. Sometimes I was running around the outside of a huge building. Over and over. Just sprinting around the building, scared and trying to escape. I would wake up terrified and sweating. I was so unsettled. I told both Esteban and Britney about the dreams I was having. At times I would be driving home from work and feel paranoid. I looked over my shoulder and peered into all the cars around me. Trying to ignore this uncanny feeling that someone was watching me. It was incredibly unnerving. The dreams weren't random. I knew something was going on but I had no idea what. I didn't lead a lifestyle that would give me these types of concerns. I went from work to home. I hung out with Esteban, Britney and the kids. Who could be out to get me? One day I got a call from an old friend.

"They got him."

"What do you mean they got him?"

"Tash they got him"

I hung up and let out a blood curdling scream. I knew he was talking about Jeron. He was an ex boyfriend of mine. Someone I dated on and off for years. Even after the break up we never lost contact and always remained friends. I loved him dearly. It wasn't romantic or based on thoughts of getting back together. I realized years before that wouldn't work. Despite that he was someone I planned to have in my life forever. Two weeks prior he called me and asked

"Do you still love me?"

"I'll always love you.

"For real?"

"Come on you don't even have to ask me that."

Of course looking back I wish I said more. I had no idea it would be one of the last times we spoke. But I think he knew exactly how I felt. That I always loved him and it never stopped. We had so many experiences together. We never lost contact, over all the years. He made sure I knew that he would always love me. Despite the fact we had not been intimate since we were 18. The love we shared, transcended anything physical. But his involvement in the street life is what ended our relationship. I was scared to stay with him. He was constantly in and out of jail. He lived a life that was too much for me even in my wildest days. But he had another side that very few people got to see. He could be sensitive but life hadn't shown him that was safe. There was a level of vulnerability we shared. He often said he could tell me anything, and he did. We talked about life. We shared our pain, fears and trauma. He told me he wanted more out of life than the way he was living. We went to church together and talked about religion and the meaning of life. There was a lot of love and beauty between us. On the other hand he also shared things that scared me. He had a side I was usually shielded from. He made sure I wasn't involved in the things that he did. It was rare but there were times I caught glimpses of his anger. Once I was in my friend Natalie's car in East Oakland. We left a sideshow and were in a drive thru. We were laughing and talking when the back door got snatched open. It was Jeron. His hand was on his waist gripping a gun. We all screamed. He thought a guy in the car was someone I was talking to. I jumped out to explain I didn't even know that man. In fact, his girlfriend was in the car too. He laughed when he realized, then kissed me and left. I got back into the car still shaking. But that's how he was about me. Protective. Another time I was asleep in the passenger seat of Natalie's car. We were riding through East Oakland. I got a phone call that woke me up. "What you doing? Where you going? Have her turn that car around and come here!" He wasn't angry. He just happened to see me asleep in her car as we passed by him. He was very aware when it came to me. He was also too caught up in the Oakland life. He would get out of jail and want to parole to my house. I refused. I couldn't bring that element to my home. I certainly wasn't going to bring that around my daughter. His sister and I tried so hard to convince him to move. His father lived out the state and offered for him to come out there. He wouldn't go and actually got angry when I brought it up. I could see there was no future for him in Oakland but he refused to leave.

About a week before he died, he called and asked if he could go to church with me. I didn't take him. I was so worried about my relationship with Esteban. How could I take him to the church we attended together? How would it look and how would I explain it to Esteban? The decision not to take him haunted me for years. I didn't know it would be our last conversation. The next call I received was telling me he had been murdered. I was in agony. The dreams were trying to warn me. Why didn't I know they were about him? All the what ifs kept replaying in my mind. It threw me into a depression for months. I broke into tears at random times. The nightmares had stopped but I had difficulty sleeping. Guilt is a dangerous emotion. Forgiveness and acceptance are essential to mental health. I had to forgive myself. I had to accept that I could not change what happened. I did it eventually, but it took me some time. So much so that later on Esteban told me he postponed proposing to me. He said it didn't feel right because of the level of pain, agony and grief I was in. I went to meet with Jerons sister shortly after his death and told her about the dream. She explained that it was incredibly close to how it happened, down to what the person was wearing. He tried to run to the corner to escape. He was shot and never got up. The building in my dream was Eastmont mall. A huge mall that was directly across the street from where he was murdered.

Jeron loved "A Change Is Gonna Come" by Sam Cooke. He used to ask his best friend to sing him the lyrics when he was going through difficult times.

It's been too hard living, but I'm afraid to die

Because I don't know what's out there, beyond the sky

It's been a long, long time coming

But I know a change is gonna come, oh yes it will

I go to the movie, and I go downtown

Somebody keep telling me don't hang around

It's been a long, long time coming

But I know a change gonna come, oh yes it will

Then I go to my brother

And say brother help me please

But he winds up knocking me

Back on my knees

It's been a long, long time coming

But I know a change is gonna come

He was murdered by someone he considered a friend. His last words were Don't do it.

I can't tell you how many times I have randomly heard this song since his passing. Sometimes it pops on the radio when he's on my mind. Once, shortly after he died, I was thinking about him as I walked into a coffee shop. As I stepped inside, the soulful lyrics filled the small space. "I was borrrrnnnnnnnnn by the riverrrr". Recently, I was on the phone with a friend. I found myself reminiscing about Jeron as I shared old stories of us. I was walking into a beauty supply and told my friend I would call him back. It was silent in the store and I started picking up color and other items for the salon. Less than 5 minutes after I entered, a song blasted super loud. "Then I go to my brother, and say brother help me pleaaaase. But he winds up, knockiiing meee". It came from a music system at the security desk in the back. "Sorry!" the guard yelled out "I don't know how that happened". I smiled and whispered, I do. Jeron has his way of showing up. Our love transcends this world. We weren't meant to be together but the connection we had is deeper than I can explain. He even visited me once in a dream. We were in a car talking. He was staring straight forward. He never looked me in my face and I should have let him speak more. But I was anxious and rushing to explain.

"Why didn't you speak at my funeral?"

"I was so overwhelmed. I had been there for hours before it started. Me and your sister were the first ones there, I went inside as soon as they opened the doors. I was sick with pain. I couldn't stop crying. I'm so sorry. I had no idea the dream was about you. I wish I would have known. I would have warned you." He stared straight ahead.

There were so many more things I wish I would have said. I hope he knew. I think he was tired of this life and his spirit was ready to move on. He never visited in another dream. But his sister gave me a small urn with his ashes. Every now and then I pull them out and rub them, hoping he's happier where he is now.

I slowly started to heal and forgive myself in the months after Jeron's murder. But like any pain, it took some time. It affected my mood and didn't help my relationship with Esteban. I don't know how we went from being so perfect to things being so difficult. But anything worth having takes work. People give up when things get hard. Yet so often success is right around the corner. We were going through a rough patch, but one that was worth fighting through. Thankfully the time apart in Spain was good for our relationship. We used the next few months to come back together stronger. You've got to grow through what you go through. That applies individually and as a couple. We focused on making our family stronger. It was a period of healing and growth. Life began to get better. Soon we were back in a great place, happy and in love. About a year later he planned a beautiful Valentine's Day celebration. As he drove us to San Francisco we held hands and talked about how far we had come and all the amazing experiences we had together. We arrived at the boat cruise and met up with two other couples. I was wearing this beautiful strapless, long gray dress and he looked so dapper in his suit. After dinner we all headed to the dance floor. I must have made the wrong move because my zipper popped in the back. I grabbed Britney and Crystal, running to the bathroom in an attempt to fix my dress. We tried everything we could but it wouldn't stay together. Britney ran outside and saw a waiter, then begged him for his name tag. Surprisingly he gave it up and we used the safety pin to hold the dress the best it could. Laughing hysterically, we headed back to the men. Towards the end of the night we ended up on the top floor. As we passed under the bridge he dropped to one knee to propose. It was beautiful. In that moment all of the past pain made sense. Life isn't a fairytale. There are ups and downs. The hard parts are where we change. Those are the opportunities for growth. It all happened to get me ready for him.

Like most girls I always dreamed of a big wedding. But first we needed to have a serious conversation. We had talked about our dreams and goals and a part of that was having another child. I was starting to have some concerns about my ability to get pregnant again. I was always worried about the side effects of hormonal birth control. Because of that I avoided it since my early 20s. When I dated women birth control wasn't necessary and with a man you can use a condom. I explained my feelings to Esteban early in our relationship. He understood and within the first year we stopped all forms of birth control. We weren't trying to get pregnant but we also weren't trying to avoid it. By now I should have gotten pregnant. I suddenly realized there was a possibility I wouldn't be able to have more children, or it might be extremely difficult. Infertility is something a lot of women struggle with so I wasn't ashamed, but I needed to know where he stood. He made it clear he wanted another baby but wanted me more. Having another child was a desire but not a deal breaker. In that moment I fell deeper in love. I felt loved, accepted and seen. Before making a huge commitment we needed to be on the same page. That conversation took a huge weight off and we were ready to move forward. He demonstrated again that he was the man I wanted to marry.

The next few months were spent on Pinterest getting wedding ideas and visiting venues every weekend. I obsessed over dress designs and made Esteban watch countless episodes of Say Yes to the Dress. I read wedding blogs and compiled a list of possible songs to walk down the aisle. It is so interesting how life works. I was so deep into wedding planning that a few months passed before I realized my period was late. It was never regular but this late was unusual. I went to the doctor cautiously optimistic. I wouldn't admit it outloud, as if I would somehow jinx it, but I was hoping I was pregnant. When the test was negative I smiled and brushed it off. I went home disappointed but happy to have the distraction of wedding planning. I wouldn't admit it out loud, but a part of me felt like I was being punished for my abortion all those years ago. The negativity test result hammered in a fear that I would never get pregnant. About a month later my period still hadn't arrived. I went to the store and purchased one of those Clear Blue pregnancy kits. As soon as I arrived home I went straight to the bathroom. Both tests were negative. I stuffed them back in the box and hid it towards the bottom of the garbage. I was embarrassed. Like there was something wrong with me. Friends got pregnant so easily and for me it was such a struggle. A few weeks later I made another doctor's appointment. The doctor ordered another test, which again was negative. They prescribed medication to restart my period. I took it and waited. A week later, still nothing. I was frustrated but had total faith in God's plan. What's meant to be will be. However, God helps those who help themselves. So, I did my research and discovered Maca root. It has been used for centuries to regulate women's hormones and increase fertility. I started taking it every morning. Another month went by and still nothing. At this point I was thinking what the fuck is wrong with me? Natural didn't work and medicine didn't work. I decided to try a different doctor. I found one in an affluent area, hoping to be taken seriously and get some results. I drove to Danville for my first visit, as soon as I arrived they asked me to take another pregnancy test.

"Ma'am I've taken about 5 tests. I am not pregnant"

"I know I know" she responded "We just need to have it on file for this office". She then prescribed me a double dose of Medroxyprogesterone. "That will bring your period back. In the meantime would you like to wait for the results?"

"No thank you" I laughed.

"Please just have a seat. We will give you the results and then book your next appointment".

I was irritated. I didn't want to wait to hear the same bad news. Every negative pregnancy test was a disappointment. A wave of emotions I was in no mood to experience again. A few minutes later the nurse poked her head out. "Natasha Ickes can you come back to my office please." Uh oh. As I walked down the hall my legs felt wobbly. "Please have a seat" Oh shit. "I know this may be a bit of a shock, but congratulations. You are pregnant. We would like you to take a blood test to see exactly how far along you are. You can take the test today and come back in a few weeks for a follow up appointment". I could barely speak. I was so confused. When did I get pregnant? How could five tests be wrong? I was in a daze as I walked to my car. I immediately called Britney, and then Esteban who was in a meeting. I sat in the car, staring in the distance. My phone rang. A nurse said "Ma'am, where did you go? We have to do your blood work." In my shock I had forgotten about that. I walked back inside to finish my appointment. When I returned to my car for the second time, I realized I left my keys in the ignition. Shaken and disoriented, I drove home. The very next day I got a call asking me to return to the doctor. The nurse said my HCG numbers were extremely high and she wanted to do an ultrasound. At this point I had no idea what to expect. Everything was a blur. The nurse gasped and I almost fell off the table. There was a whole baby inside of me. Not the little dot you normally see at the first ultrasound. I could easily identify the arms, legs and head. It was the strangest feeling. They estimated I was about 4 months. The same time when I had the abortion years ago. I was happy, scared and excited all at once. My spirit told me it was a boy. However the gender was irrelevant, I just wanted a healthy baby. The power of the human body is amazing. Despite thinking I was not pregnant, I was carrying myself almost as if I was. I stopped smoking in Spain. I only had alcohol a handful of times. We even took a road trip, where I chose not to drink the entire time. I was craving asparagus and eating bushels of it as a snack. So, despite not taking prenatal vitamins, I was getting folate directly from my food. I decided to focus on that instead of fears and anxieties. I was confident that my baby would be ok.

We decided to postpone our wedding. I tucked the gorgeous gown I bought in the back of my closet and shifted my focus. Now we were planning for a baby instead. There was so much to celebrate. A few weeks later we were having a barbeque to celebrate the big news. As always, I was doing too much. Never one to sit still I cooked for the party. I was constantly moving, cleaning and serving everyone. At some point I stepped away from the guests to use the bathroom. I was on the toilet and chatting with Britney. All of a sudden, I felt a gush of blood. It was thick, bright red and terrifying. I screamed and Britney instructed me to hang up and call my doctor immediately. When I did, I was informed that I was probably having a miscarriage. There was nothing I could do to stop it. It was overwhelming and my emotions were running high. I found out I was pregnant only a few weeks before. We had excitedly shared the news with family, friends and clients. I couldn't believe I could be losing my baby already. In the middle of the barbeque, I laid down and cried. I did not leave the bed until the next day when Esteban and the girls drove me to the doctor. They offered to come inside with me but it was something I needed to do alone. If I was going to hear I lost my child, I needed space to grieve. I went inside slowly, petrified of what the ultrasound would show. As I eased myself onto the table I was prepared for the worst. I prayed over and over again. God, please let my baby be ok. When I looked at the monitor my baby's arm was in the air as if giving us a wave. My child was letting us know that everything was fine. The ultrasound tech started laughing and I burst into tears, rubbing my belly with relief. At that moment I wished I had the whole family in the room with me. I thanked God again and again.

Outside of extreme exhaustion, the rest of the pregnancy was uneventful. I worked up until the day before I went into labor. I planned to have a natural birth but knew not to have any expectations. Life has a way of laughing at our plans. I wanted to have a water birth but that went out the window when I was induced. As soon as I arrived, I was put on Pitocin and a monitor. So much for natural labor. At least it was quicker than with Kamaya. I was in labor with her for 37 hours. This time it was a total of 26 hours, 15 of which were without pain management. I started by playing soothing music and practicing deep breathing techniques. After 12 hours that was out the window and I was screaming for an epidural. I begged the nurse for help. She informed me the anesthesiologist was dealing with an emergency. After an hour I told Esteban if he didn't find and bring him to my room, he would be leaving the hospital single. Once I got an epidural, things were so much more relaxed. In between pushes I was chatting with my doctor about her recent trip to Paris. The icing on the cake was my mother being there with me. Over the years we had gotten so close. We spoke on the phone at least once a day and it meant a lot for me to have her there. My dad was there too, right outside the room, waiting to come in. After 25 minutes of pushing there he was. Esteban Jr. A huge 10 pound baby that snuggled up to me and made me feel like all was right in the world.

He was the cutest baby and I enjoyed every minute with him. He had such a pleasant personality. By 6 months he was a flying pro, having traveled all over the country for cheer competitions. So, about a year after I gave birth, I was excited to surprise Esteban with an all expense paid trip for his 38th birthday. And I was comfortable that Junior would handle the trip well. This time the family was heading to the Dominican Republic. It is his birthplace and somewhere he had been wanting to visit for some time. When we arrived we rented a car and drove across the island, enjoying the four hours from Santo Domingo to Punta Cana. We stopped to take pictures and eat at small food stands. Tiny shacks in the middle of nowhere had some of the most flavorful food I've ever experienced. We had an amazing time. I was able to practice my broken Spanish and the kids got to see where he was from. I loved the energy and vibe of the people. The pulse of the island was unique. One day we decided to spend time on the beach. It was a windy day, which was a welcome relief from the heat and humidity. Esteban, Junior and I were on a blanket eating and building sandcastles. The girls ran along the edge of water gathering seashells. Esteban yelled out as a gust of wind snatched my money and blew it away. I jumped up intent on retrieving the cash. Esteban and I were running and snatching pesos out of the air, focused on recovering as much of it as possible. That's when I heard Kamaya scream "Juniorrrrrrrr!!!". I spun around and looked towards the water. I only saw Kamaya and Jasmine. They were up to their knees in water. Kamaya's mouth was open and her eyes were wide. Her head whipped back and forth, looking frantically in every direction. She bent forward, feeling the space around her feet, desperately grabbing for something she couldn't see. Jasmine was a few feet away, also grasping at the water. They were both coming up empty handed. I looked around and it hit me. She was feeling for Juniors body on the shore. He must have taken off running towards the beach when we ran after my money. He was nowhere to be seen. I have never been more scared in my life. It was like the world stopped. I took off running as fast as I could, so petrified I couldn't even think. My mind was empty, the only focus was to make it to the water. Both Kamaya and Jasmine were still yelling his name. He hadn't surfaced. Right before I reached the shore Kamaya stumbled across his body and yanked him out of the ocean. I reached them a split second later and snatched him out of her arms. He was choking and gasping for air. Water was gurgling out of his mouth and his lips had a purple hue. I turned him over and slapped him on the back as he threw up water. Junior was confused, scared and crying. But thank God he was ok. Kamaya was crying and screaming 'Mommy he was here. He was just here. Before he could get to me the water pulled his feet out from under him. That's all I saw before he went under!" Tears were flowing as she continued "I kept looking and looking. Mommy I couldn't find him! I looked down and saw his hair, he was face down, oh my God I didn't know if he was alive." I wanted to scream, but instead kept thanking God he was alive. So many people get pulled out to sea and most don't come back alive, adults included. My body was shaking and I felt as if my legs were going to give way. My heart was pounding and I gripped him as tight as I could. I tried to steady my breath but couldn't. I was in shock that he almost got dragged out to sea. By getting sidetracked for just a few minutes, we could have lost my baby. I didn't know **CPR**. A few more seconds under the water, if Kamaya would not have found him, my child could have died. I am never able to recall that story without tearing up. I thank God continually for his grace, mercy and protection. I was so grateful for Kamaya being guided to his body. At 10 years old she saved his life. At first, after that, Junior was scared of the water. He didn't even want to get near it. By the end of the trip he was right back to jumping in the ocean, this time with a tight grip on my hand.

Overall life felt perfect. I had all I wanted and needed. My family, our health and safety, a great career and lots of love. True to life, perfection can't last. There were some things I had been avoiding for far too long. Things I had stuffed down hoping they would disappear. Time was about to run out. Of course, there rough moments were going to be the pathway to some great ones.

Live life as if everything is rigged in your favor.

-Rumi

Chapter 9- Nowhere to Run

You can't run forever and you don't get to pick and choose what parts of yourself to fix. At some point you have to deal with your shit. Often with more consequences than if we addressed them head on. The longer you wait the harder it gets. That is universal to all issues. Ignoring problems in your marriage will eventually result in cheating, divorce or mutual misery. Ignoring confusion in a class will produce low grades. Ignoring your health will lead to diabetes, high blood pressure or another serious disease. Any addictions ignored, will only grow. I understood this and had let go of most of my addictions. But there were two I hadn't been able to break. Those lingering ones, left unaddressed, could no longer be avoided.

Sweat was dripping down my face. It was before noon and my shirt was already sticking to my back. The thick air made it hard to breathe, but on the bright side my headache was finally subsiding. The heavy thump thump thump from earlier was now a softer tap. The morning started out pretty ordinary. At some point, well before my series of alarms began to wake up the house, I was staring at the ceiling. In, out, in, out. In, out, in, out. Deep breaths with the specific intention of keeping down last night's dinner. It seemed like every morning started the same, tossing and turning, trying to press my face into the sheets in an attempt to minimize the pounding in my head. This morning was slightly worse than average. It felt like someone was hitting the right side of my face with a sledgehammer. I kept gently rubbing my temples until I drifted off to sleep, only to pop right back up from the pain. I finally reached over to the small dresser next to the bed and fumbled around until I felt it. The small, almost empty bottle of Excedrin that was always within reach. I shook out one of the last few pills, swallowed it with a swig of water and dropped my head on the pillow in relief. Less than two hours later I was running through the house engaged in our frantic morning routine. Grab your coat! Get dressed! Brush your teeth! Don't forget to pack lunch! Help get your brother ready for school please! Let me shower in peace!

It was always a mad dash to pull out my driveway before 7am. It was the magical cut off that determined if we were going to have a relaxed easy drive. Leaving after 7 meant hectic, bumper to bumper traffic. I prefer not to start my morning with blazing horns and angry drivers. By the grace of God that morning was a smooth 20 minute ride. The only noise was the radio and crunch of dry cereal from the back seat. We pulled up to my 4 year olds daycare before they opened. "You're going to be a good boy today right?" Junior nodded and smiled. "Ok put on your shoes". "Only after we play 1 game and sing

2 songs" he replied. I laughed and started humming our favorite song "E S T E B A N la la la, and that's how you spell Esteban". A few rounds of that before moving into Rock, paper, scissors. "How do you beat me every time?" I laughed as I opened the door to head inside. That's when it started. The crying, pleading and begging. It resulted in negotiations and eventually threats on my end. After 5 minutes I gave up. "Ok get in your car seat! You better be a good boy with me at work. I have lots of clients and won't have time to keep stopping." He nodded and agreed, happily going along with anything that allowed him to skip school and come with mommy. My youngest child, the baby of the family, always wanted to be with me. It didn't matter if it was at work or the park, he was always close by. These kids have always been my soft spot, a way of healing my own wounds. He was smiling as he buckled his car seat.

Five minutes later we were in a line of cars. Parents rushing to drop off kids reluctant to leave air conditioned back seats. Children already on the playground laughing and chasing each other. Teachers standing outside sipping coffee and keeping order. In the back seat Kamaya quietly pushed her books into her bag. Although I could tell she wished she could come with us, she was silent. That conversation had taken place enough times for her to know the answer. Missing 7th grade to sit at my job was not an option. Instead, we jumped directly into our morning ritual which was me fussing at her because she still wasn't ready when we pulled up to school. "Why aren't your shoes on? Do you have your homework? Don't forget to turn it in please. Check on your grades today. Make sure you have your phone so you can catch an Uber to the shop after school." I always felt terrible giving a list of demands. But my sweet girl couldn't remember details without constant reminders. "Have a great day, I love you!" I yelled out the window. Despite her visible irritation she yelled back "Love you too!" as her brother and I sped off.

I kept the window down to get a cool breeze. The heat wave over the last week meant an even hotter day in the salon, so I wanted to enjoy the fresh air while I could. "I'm hungry" squeaked a little voice in the back seat. I glanced at my purse full of snacks. They seemed suddenly insufficient for the full day ahead. You would think I would be prepared by now, seeing as though he came with me to work about 3 days a week. Maybe I thought today was the day he would go to school, maybe I just wanted a reason to go by the store. "Last stop honey!" I told him as we pulled up the closest corner store. By the time I grabbed my purse he was unbuckled and was ready to go. "Hey Natasha." My smile to the cashier masked the thought that I should stop coming here so often. We walked out with cereal, fresh fruit, apple juice and 4 small shots of tequila.

Junior spent the first 2 years of his life with me literally every day at work. Most of his first year was spent in a swing set or strapped to me in a carrier. Later he was crawling from client to client as they bribed him with snacks and treats. By age 4 his presence was expected. On this particular day he insisted on taking the stairs with no help and grabbed at my keys as if he was going to let us in. Junior ran straight to a pile of toy cars tucked in the corner. A few minutes later I heard the door swing open "Junior you're growing up!". Immediately after my client jumped into a story about how her husband pissed her off. We laughed and talked while I worked on her hair. As I finished up my friend Cynthia walked in and I knew we were in for some laughs. I always told her she missed her calling as a stand up comedian. True to tradition she came in ready to entertain. Salons are known for good conversation so she was right on time. Over the next hour we caught up on two weeks of gossip. By the time I started pressing her hair we had tears in our eyes from laughter. Before I knew it a few hours had passed. Only noon? My thoughts kept creeping back to the tequila shots in my purse. They were supposed to be for after work. A reward at the end of the day. I shoved the thoughts to the side. I would wait.

By the time I swallowed the first two shots I didn't care that it was barely one o'clock. I was just relieved my client walked into the bathroom long enough for me to gulp them down. I told myself it was ok, at least I turned my back so my son wouldn't see. Funny how we lie to ourselves. We see (and often judge) everyone else. But we rationalize our own behavior. Excuses are ok when it comes to ourselves. I was clearly wrong. But I chose to ignore it. I was at work (with my child) alcohol should not have been present. Beyond that, alcohol had become a crutch since I stopped weed. I had transferred addictions. I was aware of it, but had not been able to stop, The first shot quieted my mental chatter. I didn't care anymore that it was barely noon on a Monday. By the second shot I convinced myself it was better to drink it before my daughter got there. She's fiercely protective of me and would notice. As the drinks took hold I was feeling good. That temporary good where you forget all the mess. Those few moments where you numb the pain. The space in time where you forget why you are numbing yourself in the first place. I finished my client and was relieved my next client was late. Now I had time to sneak the next 2 shots. I wasn't even bothered that she was late, although that is usually a huge pet peeve for me. Really because it helps keep everything on schedule. And I like a schedule. In order to get an average of 10 clients a day done, with a toddler there and an older child joining me after school, I needed to stay on schedule. I was drinking 4 shots before 2 but God forbid a client be 10 minutes late. One of those examples of how we can see everyone's shit but our own. Be aware of what you hyper focus on. It is often a distraction from looking within. It is much easier to point out the fault in others, than to address our own issues.

We completed the day. I did ten clients and made in one day what I used to make in a week. Ignoring the voice that reminded me I was supposed to stop drinking. I focused on the fact that my daughter got her homework done and my son was happy. And even though I told myself I wouldn't, I stopped by the corner store again on the way home. I downed another shot before I got home so my husband wouldn't see. Not that he would care or judge me. He liked alcohol too. It was because I judged myself. I knew every lie I told myself was bullshit. Sad attempts to excuse my behavior and alleviate my guilt. At the time it was easier than being completely honest with myself. It was simpler to avoid the issue than to fix it. I popped a few skittle in my mouth to mask the taste, before walking in the house self conscious. I was relieved that no one seemed to notice. After dinner I told my husband I was running to the corner store to grab some ice cream. I returned home with Haagen-Dazs and another shot in my system. Everything we do serves us in some way. I wanted to be completely sober. But the alcohol silenced the voice in my head. It numbed the pain I created. By trying to avoid my issues I was in fact creating more. I had constructed a successful life. However, I was still using drugs to avoid emotions. I let go of the victim mentality years ago. But I went to the other end of the spectrum. I completely ignored and disregarded my own pain. I needed to develop a healthy way to deal with uncomfortable emotions. Numbing them does not work. When I finally went to bed that night I promised myself the next day would be different.

I stopped taking ecstasy a decade ago. I stopped weed four years earlier. Yet here I was still addicted. The behavior was the same, the drugs of choice had changed. Now it was work and alcohol. I began to ask myself what I was running from? What was it that I couldn't face? What part of reality was I trying to escape? I was still working 12-14 hour days. Overworking, talking to clients all day and neglecting my body was taking a toll. I was having major issues with my throat. I was losing my voice constantly. I found myself struggling to talk most of the time. Even on a good day it was getting more and more raspy. I was embarrassed of the way I sounded. Drinking alcohol made it considerably worse. Still, I kept drinking. Internally things were changing and my spirit was uneasy. I felt it was time to be fully clear, clean and sober. It was something I thought about daily. That is how it starts. The internal shift takes place before the external. Change your mind, change your life.

Around this time, we took a family vacation to New Orleans. We enjoyed the French Quarters. Bourbon street was fun despite covering the kids eyes from women flashing their boobs. When a fight broke out it was time to go back to the hotel. We laughed at the craziness the whole way back. It was an amazing place to explore. So much culture and good food. It started as one of our favorite family vacations. That is until the night Esteban came in after hours of gambling. He was loud, angry, incoherent and drunk. The kids were crying and I was scared. We argued until he fell asleep. He took one twin sized bed and the kids and I took the other. It was so uncomfortable that after a few hours I made my way to the floor with an extra blanket and pillow. By the morning I was furious and exhausted. He got so drunk that I never wanted to drink again. I wasn't even drinking that night. Instead, I was a witness to how clearly things needed to change for the both of us. This is how God uses pain to transform us. The pain and frustration of that evening was the direct catalyst to my change. I had the motivation but I knew I needed help. I logged onto Amazon on a search for self help books, and came across The Naked Mind. It is one of the most transformative books I have ever read. It highlighted the drinking culture in America, and the influence it has on all of us. It reminded us that alcohol is carcinogenic and one of the most dangerous drugs to consume. By the end it literally changed the way I felt about alcohol. Even more amazing, it got rid of my desire to drink. It takes a radical life changing approach that works. I was completely sober for the first time since I was 16. Before I was only sober when I was pregnant or in jail. I was so used to being on a substance that being sober was the new high.

Everything looked and felt clearer. My thoughts, words and actions were intentional. It was beautiful but I still had to develop a new approach to deal with tough emotions. I also needed to figure out why I turned to substances for so many years of my life. I needed to understand so I wouldn't repeat destructive behaviors. I had to heal from the things I was running from. It also came down to habits. Habits are easy to build and difficult to break. When I felt an uncomfortable emotion, my habit was to work or drink. If I worked 14 hours, I would be too tired to feel. Some people overeat, some people shop, some people gamble. I wanted to learn how to deal with my emotions in a positive way so I wouldn't go back to old habits.

When I took ecstasy years before it heightened my senses. Part of that was my intuition. When I was high, I felt more connected to everything. I was able to sense so many things before they happened. The reality is I experienced the same things sober. But the addict part of my mind was convinced I needed ecstasy to access that part of myself. I was scared of losing that connection. At one time I was having premonitions every week. Some of which saved my life. Intuition is defined as the ability to understand something immediately, without the need for conscious reasoning. Intuition is a gift we all have. However, everyone's gift manifests in different ways. The more we listen to our intuition, the quicker we recognize it when it appears. It's like a muscle and the more we practice tuning in, the stronger it becomes. It's important to understand not all premonitions and intuitive hits are clear cut. Mine comes in predominantly two ways. Sometimes I hear things and other times I get a strong gut feeling. A feeling so strong that I know it to be a fact. When it comes in the form of hearing it is a short simple phrase. At times it's related to something small. One evening I was driving on the freeway and heard "you're about to get pulled over". I repeated it out loud to my friends. Less than 3 minutes later we saw the lights, despite not speeding or previously seeing a cop car. Other times it's more powerful. Like the dream about Jeron, where I heard "you won't get back up" as I fell to the ground. With my high school boyfriend it happened all the time. Several times I was at home and would hear "he's cheating". I would confront him only to find out I was right. Once Helen called me about a mutual friend Alexis.

"Guess what just happened to Alexis?"

"'She called her boyfriend and another female answered the phone"

"Oh, she called and told you already" Helen laughed.

"No, she didn't"

Helen didn't believe me and called Alexis. She was informed that it just happened and Helen was the only person who knew. Helen asked me for a week how I had done it. I was honest with her that I didn't know, the information just came to me. It's not a science and I can't decide what information I will receive. My mind is not a crystal ball that I can ask any question. I am given foresight on certain things and at times I am a bit off. However, none of these incidents involved Ecstasy.

Needing a drug to enhance my intuition, was a lie I told myself.

One day I was in the salon and received a call from an old friend Rodney. He was chatting about plans to hang out with someone he had just met. I was immediately gripped with a feeling of dread. "It's a set up! Please don't go with him! You can't go with anyone you don't know tonight" Despite my seriousness he laughed. My anxiety increased after we hung up. I immediately called a mutual friend Brandon in a panic. He answered the phone sleepily. "Please call Rodney! Tell him not to go with anyone he doesn't know tonight. It's going to be a set up." Brandon was quiet and asked to call me back. Brandon is a truck driver. At the time he was on the road doing a two person run. Which means he was going cross country with another driver to make deliveries. They had been arguing the whole trip. Two men in tight quarters for an extended period of time can be stressful. It got so bad that he pulled over the truck ready to fight. The other driver didn't want to get physical, but from there on it was tension. I hadn't spoken to Brandon in over a month, so I didn't know any of this when I called. Apparently, he was in and out of sleep when he overheard his co-worker speaking in a hushed voice on the phone. He could only make out bits and pieces of the conversation. As they pulled up to the rest stop his coworker whispered "We can't do it here, there are too many people." That was the moment I called. He was trying to make sense out of what the coworker said. The fact that I called talking about a set up raised his antennas. He rushed me off the phone and told his coworker he was going to take a shower inside the rest stop. After his shower he called me back.

"Did you call Rodney?" I asked.

"Nah. I got out of the shower and the truck was gone."

"It was gone? What the fuck? How can dude just leave you at a rest stop in the middle of nowhere?"

"It's some weird shit going on here. You don't even call me like that. When was the last time you called my phone? Then you call now to say something about a set up. You woke my game up". He proceeded to fill me in on the story before continuing. "And I called him to see where he was, but he kept telling me to catch an uber to some random spot. Then I hear some dude in the background ask if I'm coming"

I asked "Who is the guy in the background?"

"Shit I don't know. This is his hometown. He knows hella people out here."

I panicked. I told him I heard "Don't go anywhere with anyone you don't know tonight". I knew I was off and it wasn't about Rodney. It was about him.

"You won't go right? Promise me you won't go."

"Man, I'm not catching an Uber over there. That would be my last damn Uber ride. This dude is trying to set me up!"

The driver refused to come back and pick him up in the truck. He asked Brandon repeatedly to go to a random location. Instead, he went to a hotel room and never saw that driver again. Although we have no proof, we are convinced the coworker was trying to have him killed. He thanked me many times after that day.

These moments were confirmation. As long as I'm open, God will guide and show me what I need to know. Drugs are not what connects me to my intuition. That was the lie I told myself, to excuse my behavior. Once my mind and body were clear, I focused on self development. I used my energy to invest in classes. I read books that fostered self-growth and development. I appreciated learning from the wins, losses and challenges of others. I was also drawn to natural healing. I became a certified Reiki practitioner. About a year later I took a Tarot course. According to Brigit Esselmont, founder of Biddy Tarot "Tarot is the storybook of our life, the mirror to our soul and the key to inner wisdom. Every spiritual lesson we meet in our lives can be found in the seventy-eight Tarot cards. And when we consult the Tarot, we'll get shown the exact lessons we need to learn and master to live an inspired life. It's like holding up a mirror to yourself so that you can access your subconscious mind. Tarot allows us to tap into the wisdom and answers that live in us all." In the beginning I was doubtful of the accuracy of the cards. However, every reading I did made me more and more of a believer. Not just for myself but for others as well. It was amazing the reactions I got. People burst into tears, let go of pain and were strengthened to take the next step in their lives. Before I knew it, I was doing weekly Tarot readings for clients at the salon. I had crystals, herbs and vitamins with coinciding books to understand their benefits. It was common to make my own tinctures and natural remedies. After years of self-destruction, I was in love with self-growth. I had been on that journey for decades. Peeling back the layers and fighting to elevate myself. Learning and growing, falling and getting back up. Becoming the healthiest person I could be in mind, body and soul. It wasn't until I was completely sober, that I felt as if it had all come together. On my journey I learned a lot of lessons.

Health is wealth. Despite being completely sober, overworking was taking a toll. I lost my voice every week and spent most days whispering. It took years before I finally went in to see what was wrong. I assumed it was just my body's reaction to fatigue. I found out I had a cyst on my vocal chord and went straight to surgery to have it removed. I didn't stop overworking. Eventually that led to daily migraines and panic attacks. I went into the doctor and my blood pressure was high. My numbers put me close to hypertension stage 1. After a brief conversation with my doctor, I walked out with four prescriptions. I filled the prescriptions but was hesitant to take any of the meds. A few days later I was sharing this with a client. I felt like the meds were a band aid to the real issue. She mentioned having migraines when she needed glasses. Two days later I had glasses, no panic attacks and my migraines had reduced by 60 percent. To combat the high blood pressure, I went vegan. It wasn't always easy, but it was worth it. Within a month my blood pressure was back in the ideal range. I never took any of the prescribed meds. I spent so many years putting dangerous substances in my body that I wanted to be as clear as possible. And I finally learned the lesson, slow down at work. Honor my body with rest.

I was living the life of my dreams, choosing to be as healthy and happy as possible. Things were going so well. Esteban and I just purchased our second home. I received an award of Congressional Recognition and was named a Woman of Valor for my volunteer work in the community. Opportunities kept pouring in. I got called to be a judge for Miss Teen USA. I even had a booth at a huge local bridal fair where I did the hair for the entire runway show. I was set up next to huge companies like Macys and couture wedding boutiques. At first I felt inadequate. That is one way the ego tries to take over. It talks us out of our blessings and makes us doubt our power. When I walked in and saw all the professional setups I was embarrassed and wanted to leave. But I had to remember my motto which is do it scared. Because if we walk away from everything that scares us, our lives will be mediocre. So, I pulled myself together. I remembered that God has my back. I walked to a local Walgreens and bought a few things to improve my setup. I took notes on how to make it better for next time. Then I walked back in there with my head held high and got to work. The show was amazing, I got tons of compliments on the hair styles I created, and I got several clients from the event. I did my best while simultaneously learning how to do it better going forward. Things were great, I was sober and I was ready to take my life to the next level. It's so easy to stop at good, because shooting for great is scary as hell. But God had more in store for me.

Start a huge, foolish project, like Noah... it makes absolutely no difference what people think of you.

-Rumi

Chapter 10- Alchemy

R ide the waves of life, you never know where they
may take you. One day my mom invited me to
hear a woman speak. As with a lot of things we
walk into, I had no idea this was getting ready to change
my life. Everything went wrong to deter me from making
it to the event. I left work later than planned. I hadn't
eaten all day and tried to get food on the way. Everywhere
I passed was closed. I gave up on food and decided to
head straight to the event. I spent 15 minutes looking for
a park. I eventually found a 2 hour park, the event was 4
hours. I decided to take a chance and just pay for two
hours. I got out and the meter was broken. But
something would not let me give up. I went in with zero
expectations and left enrolled in a 3 day retreat. She
spoke on love, life, connections, manifestation, raising
our expectations and up leveling every area of life. Topics
I had been into for years. I was in heaven. By the end of
the weekend retreat I paid $30,000 to work with Mahima
Klinge for a year. It scared me to invest that big but if you
want big results you have to go all in. Mahima herself had

been mentored by Lisa Nichols, Kane and multiple others. When she spoke I connected with her. Life was already great, but I wanted to go on a spiritual journey. Plus, everyone from Oprah to Bill Gates recommends hiring mentors. If it helped them, I could definitely benefit. There was this nagging feeling that I was on the edge of something big, but I had no idea what. I sensed that my life was about to change. At that amount of money, I was going to make sure that it did.

Within a few months of working with Mahima I had a realization. Despite my love of hair, I was put on this planet to do more. She only knew a fraction of my story and was convinced hair wasn't my lifelong purpose. I knew I survived for a reason, but I was comfortable in my career. I was grateful for all the lessons I learned and enjoyed sharing them with clients. She was convinced I was meant to pass on that knowledge in a meaningful way. She showed me how to use my mistakes, pain and trauma to help others. I considered how I could teach the tools I learned, to help other women. That's the beauty of a mentor, they see more in you than you see in yourself. I was ready. Plus, I love to facilitate transformation. In the salon that was what I enjoyed most. That was part of the joy of volunteering at shelters. Meaningful conversations. Uplifting and motivating the people I encountered. Making light of the bad and then using it as a step stool to something better. But in those settings, it was limited. I left charity events wanting to make a deeper impact. I wanted to help women use their trauma as a catalyst for success. I wanted to teach specific steps to move from pain to purpose. I discovered my what. What I was meant to do for the next stage of my life. What my impact and legacy would be. Now the question was how. The thought of changing careers was terrifying. My identity and security was tied to being a hairstylist and salon owner. That part of my life was solid. I was making around 140k annually. I enjoyed my career. However, that calling couldn't be ignored. What calling on your life, are you ignoring?

We all have an identity, a way we are viewed in the world. Too often we let others define who we are. It can be intimidating to step outside of the box people put you in. You may be CEO of a large company, but your desire is to teach yoga. It might be embarrassing to share that with your family, friends and coworkers. Actually, you could make more money teaching yoga. Why? Because when you follow your passion it will be more fulfilling and profitable than any other path. Or you may have been in banking for 20 years and then decide you want to be a teacher. Again, your circle might not be supportive. Disregard that. You deserve to be fulfilled. You could have been a cashier for the last decade but have a deep calling to be a nurse. Others may doubt your ability to change. Stay connected to your vision, knowing anything is possible. Whatever it is, you can't live for anyone else. If you want to be happy and successful you have to follow your own path. If you don't, you will be miserable. My identity was Natasha the hair stylist, Natasha the salon owner. That career took me from homeless to homeowner. It changed the trajectory of my life. In many ways it saved me. It allowed me the money and freedom to do whatever I wanted. I honored it but now I was on a new path. One that spoke to my soul, but with no financial promises. It was scary and exciting at the same time. I wanted it so bad, but I was embarrassed to share my dreams, in case they didn't happen. I had to be ok with the possibility of failure. Risk is involved in any huge reward. So, I went for it and became a certified life coach. I read the books, took the classes and put in the work. Luckily, I would be teaching skills I spent decades learning and practicing myself. I began coaching clients. I was nervous at first. Then I was amazed at the transformations I saw taking place. Next, I developed an online course to go with 1-1 coaching. I shared the blueprint that saved my life. Within a year I hired a top business coach Kane. His company Start At the Top worked with everyone from Kevin on Shark Tank to Les Brown. I am currently planning a wellness retreat. A healing space filled with love, light and transformation. This is just the beginning of this leg of my journey. I have already had some disappointments. I sulked for a few hours, then got over it. I learned the lessons to be better going forward.

Looking back, I thank God for the pain. Affliction is a part of life. We all experience struggles, they prepare us for greatness. Look at an Olympian. They outwork thousands of athletes to get to that level. They sacrifice and push their bodies to the extreme. It is through hard work, dedication and pain that they develop the skills to win. The same goes for every area of life. There is no limit to success when you grow through what you go through. You can not fail if you keep trying. The big secret is not to give up. The saddest thing is to stay in a negative space. That is where you draw out the pain and turn it into suffering. Don't lose sight of the bigger picture. Transformation is ongoing, evolution is never ending and learning is a lifelong process.

Without specific tools we stay way too long in the valleys of life. How do you respond to disappointment? Do you learn the lessons and become stronger or do you stay in the pain? Are you the type to be hurt once, and then give up? Do you shut down after one heartbreak? Do you find yourself not taking chances because you are scared? Living a mediocre life to avoid failure. Not realizing you aren't avoiding pain, you are only changing the type of pain you will experience. Let's say you want to be a lawyer. You could take the risk and go for it. That means school, probably loans and a very difficult bar exam. All without the guarantee of success. But at least, at the end of the day, knowing you gave it your all. And the odds are you would be incredibly successful. The other option is to take the easy route, to avoid the possibility of failure. Instead of going for your dream you could work at a retail store. There isn't much risk, but there also isn't much reward. You would trade the pain of years of schooling, for the pain of a low income. In addition, you would live with the pain of not pursuing your passion and your purpose. Pain is unavoidable, you decide which kind to experience. It is much better to give it your all and experience the pain that comes on your way to success, than to live a life of mediocrity. On my journey of transformation and growth thus far, I learned, honed and developed some skills that made life easier. It is these life lessons that are the premise of what I call the Dream Formula. It is how we let go of being stuck, depressed and unfulfilled. It is how we step out of pain, fear and mediocrity. It is a step by step guide to develop a consistent peace, power and purpose. It is a blueprint to living our greatest potential.

Peace isn't an abstract, unattainable concept. True peace starts with accepting yourself, wherever you are in your journey. The goal is a peace that's independent of outside people, circumstances and situations. No one should have control over your emotions. A rude cashier, a flat tire, even losing your job should not affect your peace long term. If outside sources have the power to make you happy, they also have the power to make you sad. When you control your emotions, peace is sustainable. A part of peace is accepting any outcome. Acceptance is a result of trusting the process. Let's say you have a job interview at your dream company. Peace is being ok no matter what happens. You prepare and give it your all. But you trust in the universe, knowing that if you don't get it, there is a better opportunity waiting. In order to maintain peace, control what you can and be ok with the rest. It takes a specific mindset, perspective and practice to attain. But once you do it's priceless.

You are powerful. The power I am referring to comes from within. It's derived from love, acceptance and forgiveness. It grows every time you demonstrate these attributes towards yourself and others. It is the power that comes from a connection to the spirit. It gives you the confidence to know, that even when it's hard you can continue to push through. What is your purpose? Your divine reason for being on this planet. Why are you here? What legacy are you going to leave behind? How will you live so that at the end of it all you have no regrets? If you're not sure, get a journal. Write daily. Meditate. Hire a mentor. Join a program that helps you discover all of those things. Mark Twain said "The two most important days of your life are the day you are born and the day you figure out why".

I would like to leave you with the five steps that helped me create the life of my dreams. No matter what your aspirations, they can help you elevate your life and achieve your goals.

1. **Discover-** Go within to discover who you are and what you want. Take time to identify your true self. You must do the work to discern who you are versus who the world wants you to be. Who are you beyond your job, money and titles? Do you like what is left? You must discover your passion and reveal your purpose. In this stage a great exercise is to daydream and write down your goals. Ask yourself what would you do if you knew you would not fail? Think big. Hint: if it doesn't scare you then you are playing it too safe. Focus on what you want. Throw away the how. Too often we use logic and reason to talk us out of our dreams. Anything is possible, the only limits are those of our imagination. In this exercise take your time and encompass every area of your life. What do you envision for your relationship, family, health, career, fun and finances. Write it all down so you have a starting point. When you take the active step of speaking your desires into the universe, it has a way of conspiring to make it happen.

2. **Reflect**- In order to move through life in a healthy, happy and positive way, you have to get down, dirty and honest. We all have some painful work to do. This is the stage where you do some frank self-reflection. In order to create the life of your dreams, you must first honor

and heal the trauma of your past. This is actually my favorite part. I teach my clients how to turn their pain into ART. They learn how to <u>a</u>nalyze, <u>r</u>eframe and <u>t</u>ransform every difficult situation. What is the most painful experience of your life? I mean the most agonizing, heartbreaking thing you have gone through. Look at it, hold it, sit with it. Cry, scream or be silent. It's uncomfortable to stay in that space. But it's important. After you honor the emotions, find 2-3 good things that were a direct result of the pain you experienced. I know it's difficult and counter intuitive. But you can do it.

Personal examples:

<u>Pain</u>: My divorce was traumatic. I promised myself I wouldn't raise my children in a broken home. Yet I divorced Ricky when Kamaya was 2, the same age my parents split up. On top of that Ricky has not been a consistent parent and I am watching my daughter go through an incredible amount of pain as a result.

Benefits:

1) I left a marriage that was never going to be what either one of us needed. I then became stronger because of all I went through.

2) I threw myself into work and my income doubled within a few months.

3) I learned so much about myself and how to be a better person. By being the sole parent 95% of the time our relationship is incredibly close.

Pain: A close friend stole thousands of dollars from me.

Benefits:

1) I gained an immense appreciation for my real friends like Jasmine Griffin, Brandon, Natalie, Jasmine Hicks, Max, Elias, Britney, Noel, Kia, Jessie, Mary, Sunshine, Nake and Aisha. I could keep going. Those were the relationships I needed to foster.

2) I gained the wisdom to let go when it was time. I learned to stop hanging on to dead situations.

3) I was reminded to be more careful with my money and belongings

Pain: My abortion. Taking the life of my own child is an agony I have never fully recovered from.

Benefits:

1) I gained the self-awareness to know that I could never do that again and the motivation to be the best mother possible when the time came.

2) I gained so much compassion for any woman going through that situation (regardless of her final decision).

3) I learned how to forgive myself, and that was one of the most powerful lessons of my life.

ART is about consciously shifting out of a victim mindset. It is based on the understanding that we always have a choice. We will make some good decisions and some bad ones. We must both take responsibility for the fact that we have created our reality, while also forgiving ourselves for our mistakes. It is a conscious shift from a negative to positive mindset. We can't control everything. What we can control is how we view our circumstances. We are responsible for our mindset, perspective and reactions. Happiness is a choice. What will you choose?

3. **Evolve**- This takes applied application. I like to use growth challenges to put the new mindset into practice. The purpose is to use the pain as a catalyst for change and growth. We've got to grow through what we go through. There should be a constant evolution of mind, body and spirit. Focus on your total wellness. Work out. Drink water. Sleep. Laugh. Create balance in your life. Intensify your intuition. Be aware of your energy. Mahima always says that energy flows where attention goes. You get more of what you focus on. If you focus on the negative, that is what you will get. If you move through life with the belief that everyone is mean, that will be your reality. If you believe most people are inherently good, you will see their light. Focus your thoughts. Elevate your mind, words and then actions. From there your life will change.

4. **Alignment**- Know yourself well enough to know what you want, who you want to be and how you want to live. Then do the work to make it happen. Create the steps to make your dreams come true. The path is different for everyone however the principles are the same. Have a plan. Then show up consistently, work

hard and refuse to give up. Have a supportive team around you. People that motivate you. Hire a mentor to fast track your success.

5. **Manifestation** This is the fun part. We use the tools around us to create the life of our dreams. With the help of our network, clients, coworkers, friends, coaches and mentors we make it happen. We are unstoppable when we combine our magic, with the energy and magic of the universe. We all deserve to live the life of our dreams. The heart and soul of this program is to make that happen for as many people as possible.

The common misconception about success is that it is a destination. Nope! It's a journey. Full of ups and downs, failures, lessons and success. Failure is only a punishment if you don't learn from it. No matter how much you mess up you have to keep going. I'm grateful to be on this journey, this evolution, to the best version of me. You too are on that journey. Be kind and gentle. Forgive a lot. Focusing on mistakes fills us with unnecessary anger and shame. The reality is that we will continue to fall and get back up for the rest of our lives. So, in the process hold your head high and keep trying to be better. Sometimes it's scary and that's ok. All the good stuff is scary. Love, relationships, new jobs, adventure, having children. How boring would life be if we only did the things that don't scare us. Let's look at fear as a good sign. That means we are stretching ourselves. From now on when a big opportunity comes up, do it scared. I want to leave you by re asking this question. What would you do if you knew you would not fail? That my friend, is the life you are meant to live.

It is not the critic who counts, not the one who points out how the strong man stumbles, or where the doer of deeds could have done them better

The credit belongs to the man who is actually in the arena, whose face is marred by dust and sweat and blood; who strives valiantly; who errs, who comes short again and again

Because there is no effort without error and shortcomings...

Who spends himself at a worthy cause, who at the best knows in the end the triumph of high achievement

Who at the worst, if he fails, at least fails while daring greatly

So that his place shall never be with those cold and timid souls who neither know victory nor defeat

-Theodore Roosevelt

Acknowledgments

D ad (Kyle Ickes): Thank you for an unwavering support. For showing me the true meaning of unconditional love, sacrifice and presence. I grew up knowing you had my back no matter what, no questions asked. Without you I would have been lost. Your dedication to your kids is unmatched and you are appreciated. I hope my children feel that same level of support from me.

Mom (Trisha Ickes): Thank you for teaching me so many lessons along the way. Hard work, persistence, the importance of extracurriculars and the need to focus on education. Despite a rocky start, you became one of my best friends. Thank you for being there literally anytime I call (which is everyday). Your constant feedback and support during the writing of this book was amazing. Thank you for being the best grandmother my children could ask for.

Kenny: You are a real life superhero. Thank you for being a second dad. I can't count how many times you have saved the day. You are the keeper of all my secrets and my kids best friend. I can't imagine this life without you.

Grandma Mary Logan: Thank you for instilling two of my greatest gifts, my moral compass and my connection to God. At my lowest points, your words played through my mind. Thanks to you, my children know your character is who you are when no one is looking. You are an inspiration to us all.

Esteban Saman: My husband, my rock, my love. Thank you for never giving up on me or our family. Even at the hardest moments, your love and support is unwavering. Thank you for being my tech support, round the clock ear and constant motivator. Your feedback helped make this book possible.

Kamaya: You are my first child. My rock. My little best friend. You are so beautiful, talented, intelligent and sweet. I thank God for you everyday. Remember you can literally do anything you set your mind to. Continue to shine bright.

Junior: My sweet little boy. You are brilliant. Your contagious energy, amazing laugh and bright personality are such a joy to be around. I thank God for allowing me to be your mommy.

Jasmine: Thank you for being my bonus daughter. It's been such a joy watching you grow into the smart, beautiful, talented young lady you are today. I am grateful for our journey and growth together. Continue to sparkle.

My dear brother Jesse, you inspire me in so many ways. Despite being a little brother, your courage, creativity and sense of adventure are something I look up to. Noel you were always like a sister to me. Thank you for being there for me no matter what the circumstances. Kia and Auntie Jay, you both have inspired me so much over the years. Britney you are the best friend I could ever ask for. Over 25 years of friendship, the one friend I know will never leave my side. To all my clients (there are too many to name) you have become like family. Mahima and Kane for mentoring me and helping me surpass my own expectations. I have been blessed with so many guardian angels. I have encountered great people, who have helped me along my journey. To everyone, there are so many I haven't named, I love and appreciate you.

Made in the USA
Las Vegas, NV
01 September 2021

29389829R00142